A Barefoot Journey

LINDA CHAMBERLAIN

DEDICATION

To all the horses who helped me understand their quiet
language and made this book possible.

REVIEWS FOR LINDA CHAMBERLAIN'S NOVEL THE FIRST VET

I have no hesitation in recommending this as an interesting and informative historical read. The author writes with great conviction and enthusiasm

HISTORICAL NOVEL SOCIETY

I devoured this book. A well-crafted tale

VANESSA WEBSTER, AUTHOR AND REVIEWER

Intertwining historical fact, interesting characters and a fictional love story, this is a must-read for anyone who loves horses. Really enjoyed it!

NATURAL HORSE MAGAZINE

ACKNOWLEDGMENTS

Thanks to my editor Elizabeth Bailey for keeping me on the straight and narrow. My family for putting up with me. My brilliant photographer, Will Jessel, for a great cover and Ben Catchpole for the design. That's the team.

And since I'm mentioning the cover, I must thank my elderly horse, Carrie. It is only fitting that the mare who tested my skills so much should get the starring role. We are photographed on the top of a rocky outcrop and, as she famously enjoys nudging people with her head, it's a wonder that she didn't shove me over the top. Perhaps she likes me…

CHAPTER 1

I've made it a policy to avoid arguing with well-muscled men wielding a hammer and nails. I'm not a tall woman, more a lightweight who can be pushed over easily, but my stand off with the farrier that day required me to get in touch with my masculine side. Quickly.

You see, my requirements were simple – take the shoes off my two horses since it was not a job I could do myself. He shouldn't have started a fight over it but he was jangling a set of new shoes in his hand and he wanted to fit them. I wanted him to put them in the back of his van and drive off – once he'd taken the old set off, of course.

He was a nice guy – young, lovely smile and the well-defined muscles of his trade but he had an understandable desire to keep hold of his business. Even in the face of some daft woman who had read a tiny but controversial book about riding barefoot horses. That book had shocked me and it was impossible to forget its dire warning that nailing shoes onto the hoof was slowly killing the animals we loved.

'They won't manage without them,' he said, rubbing his chin and eyeing the sad state of Barnaby's feet.

My daughter's pony made him sigh but he wrenched the old and worn shoes from her feet, gave her a trim and was ready to smooth her hooves with the heavy rasp that he could wield like a nail file. He straightened his back, swept his hair from his head with one easy swipe and came to a decision without meeting my eye.

'We'll put shoes on their fronts; that's the answer.'

This guy was one of the nicest farriers around and we had spent a few hours over the years chatting about horses and drinking tea. He had been a competitive rider when he was younger and handled the animals with sympathy and understanding. It was terribly hard to find the words to tell him that farriers had become second to undertakers on my people-to-avoid-while-alive list. If only they would retrain and become barefoot trimmers.

He went to the back of his blue van without waiting for my answer and was about to start up the furnace of his mobile forge. Years ago, we used to ride for miles to take a horse to the blacksmith but now the old forges have become bijoux dwellings and farriers drive these vans with a little gas furnace in the back so they can hot shoe horses in their own homes. The smell of burnt hoof follows them like an invisible mist.

'Oh, dear. No, I'd rather keep them all off, if you don't mind,' I said.

My voice was a bit too high pitched to be taken seriously. It needed measured base tones for men to sit up and listen. So the first attempt didn't quell the gas flame.

He wasn't listening. These horses should be barefoot. We were only riding on Ashdown Forest where there were thousands of acres of woods and heathland only an hour from London. There was hardly any road work, so surely they didn't need metal wrapped around their feet.

'Nah, his feet will crumble. Look at that crack all the way up his foot. White feet; they're all the same. Weak and useless. He'll never go barefoot.'

Barnaby had carted me around for the last five years; he was as strong as an ox and pulled like a tank. Countless osteopaths had bemoaned the state of my weary and pulled shoulders and every farrier that came within two yards of him warned me his feet were his only weak point. They cracked, they didn't grow quickly enough and so they were full of nail holes with nowhere to fix a new shoe.

His feet were in a sorry state even though he'd received all the care that conventional wisdom had advised. Dutiful and regular shoeing every six weeks. It didn't seem to be working, his feet were getting worse and he was unlikely to make it into old age as a ridden horse. Barefoot was being mooted as more than an alternative…it was a cure. That crack on my boy's near hind was caused by shoeing according to my reading and his feet were destined to get worse the longer he walked on metal instead of padding on his own feet.

It might have been the hammer that did it; then again the sight of the nails goaded me. Sharp and shining. Lined up neatly in their trays ready to be driven into Barnaby's feet if this man had his way - consigned to the history books if I had mine.

One word was all it needed. A two-lettered one.

'No.' He was listening to me properly at last and I carried on. 'We don't ride them very much. We don't compete, you know, so they'll be fine. We don't want the shoes on.'

Frankly, I would have chosen not to ride if it meant driving nails into their feet every few weeks. My new-found cause meant I was brimming with facts like a cynic who'd found God on Facebook.

This is the crux of it – the hoof is a moving part of the horse. It is NOT a block of wood. In its natural state, the hoof acts as a shock absorber by flexing on landing, it supports the heart by pumping blood back around the body and it can't work as nature intended wearing a metal shoe. Nailing metal onto a moving part of a horse causes injuries, shrinks their feet and gives them life-threatening diseases but we've been doing it for so long we're blind to the harm.

The trouble is that the hoof appears immobile to the human eye. It appears as unmoving as a pair of coconut shells slapped together to mimic the sound of a horse trotting. But if you ever get a chance, grab a barefoot horse by the leg and give his foot a squeeze. Or get someone like me to do it for you. There's a central groove on the underside of the hoof and if you press hard on the sides you can see it crease.

Better still, go on the internet and watch the films of barefoot horses in motion and see how the foot spreads when it lands, how the sole descends, how the part called the frog touches the ground.

If only the horse had a repertoire of facial expressions like a dog. Don't forget that the metal shoe is nailed on when his foot is not weight bearing. It's been lifted from the ground and is at its most narrow.

Why won't the horse frown? Or wince? Or shake his foot as though his trainers are too tight? He doesn't do any of those things but he walks in a new way that people become accustomed to. His feet are heavier and they can't flex. The only warnings for a rider who isn't listening or watching for the changes are the potential health problems further down the line.

One lone vet from Germany, Dr Hiltrud Strasser, was swimming against the tide and saying our horses' lives were being shortened dramatically by the practice of shoeing. She warned that the average age of a euthanized horse was about eight years old so my two had already passed their sell-by date. Most horses that are put to sleep are lost through lameness and, according to Dr Strasser, most lameness is caused by shoeing.

Her book was deeply moving and made me feel terribly guilty. I had owned horses since the age of fifteen. My first horse had been with me for twenty years and naturally she was shod. Had she been harmed?

Yes!

She'd suffered from painful foot problems and had been put to sleep at the age of twenty six. It was considered a good age but with hindsight she would have been more comfortable without landing on metal with every step. We might even have found a cure and enabled her to live for longer.

There was no turning the clock back but what about the future for the two we had now? Well, they couldn't live forever but I was going to give it my best shot. They shouldn't have to suffer this acceptable cruelty.

These revolutionary thoughts stayed inside me; I didn't like to hurt my farrier's feelings by repeating them.

'Well, what am *I* going to do?' he asked, eyeing me angrily.

He seemed shaken but he was only losing two horses from his list; he wouldn't miss them, would he? Of course, *I* liked them, but surely he hadn't got attached on such a short acquaintance. His face was tight as if he needed to hold onto his teeth. Embarrassment crept inside me.

'What do you mean?'

'I lose the business then? Is that it?'

'Perhaps you could still trim them for me.' There was an apology in my voice but it didn't ease his annoyance.

This was nearly fifteen years ago. A set of shoes cost about £45 and here was a job offering him £10 or £20 per horse every six weeks at the most. It wasn't much and he knew it. These horses would need trimming but his business was shoeing. To his mind, it was better for the horse to wear metal shoes since the perceived wisdom was, and still is in conventional circles, that they protect the foot. It was also better for his pay packet.

The little veterinary book that set me on this journey warned against getting the farrier to trim their feet. They trim the feet, it said, to fit a horse shoe rather than set a horse up for his barefoot life. But, there weren't many specialist barefoot trimmers in Britain at that time – I had heard of only one and she lived more than a hundred miles away – so who else would look after their feet?

It was looking more and more likely that this guy wouldn't be coming back for my measly few pounds.

He flung the rasp to the ground. As an act of intimidation, it was working. I was getting nervous. He wouldn't look at me and turned away with a hunch of his shoulders. He thought me daft and yet I understood and sympathised but was too English, too polite to tell him my views on shoeing. Perhaps we both knew that I would be the first of many owners who would take this step.

Neither of us could have envisaged that we were witnessing one of the first cracks in a tradition of metal shoeing that has held sway for more than a thousand years; a crack that would grow, with or without my contribution, into a worldwide movement affecting thousands of horses. There would be prosecutions, vilification and plenty of hatred. But there would be no stopping the change that was coming.

Horse shoeing. My farrier thought it was essential. Some thought it was killing the animals in our care. The middle ground argued it was a necessary evil.

We stood eyeing each other. Waiting. The horse owner had the upper hand in this scenario. He *had* to do the job demanded of him. Take off the shoes and trim their feet. Nothing more. Or someone else would do it.

So, of course he did and he left me with promises of a return visit that was never to happen. My horses – Barnaby, a black and white 10-year-old cob, and the small-but-perfectly-formed pony, Girlie - were barefoot. And I was on my own.

CHAPTER 2

Horses can't talk. But they can swear. The three of us stood there watching the farrier accelerate down the drive and I chewed my lip at the sight of his shaking head.

Barnaby and Girlie didn't move. The big fella had a habit of sniffing your footwear to see whether you were a rider or not; he still does it now. It's his way of getting to know you and is rather endearing. He lowered his head and had a good look at my boots.

'Are you trying to tell me it's unfair?' I said. 'OK, no riding. Not for a while.'

He could have been muttering about my comfort but his command of English was insufficient to give me a guilt trip.

'It's autumn, the ground will be soft. This is to help you, not me.'

He looked at his own feet and took a few tentative steps. His movements were apprehensive. He wasn't in pain, surely; he hadn't done anything on them yet but taking the shoes off a horse is said to be like putting your frozen, cold hands into a bucket of warm water. The sensation is described as a sudden rush of feeling. How anyone knows these things I've no idea but it's a fair guess since horse shoes numb the foot.

He walked and the pony followed. Their owner felt excited. I'd done it!

In reality, I'd done nothing but take the decision and give the order. There was a heavy weight of responsibility upon me and the world out there was hostile. There is nothing more conventional than the British horse world – I was once told that only 'travellers and the hideously poor' failed to shoe their horses. How would we justify it if they went lame? Would they manage? Would we ever ride again?

No one knew the answers but I couldn't put metal shoes back on. There was only one way out and that was forward.

With a light heart, I led those two back up the track to turn them out. Had I known what was ahead of me I might have taken a few deep breaths but foresight was notably absent. They kept to the edge where the earth was softer and they were walking differently and with care.

They could feel. They could feel in a way they hadn't felt in years. Every stone and every bit of wood was now something they needed to take into account. Their feet were soft and they were damaged by years of shoeing, they had lost much of the flexibility that their wild cousins take for granted.

It takes nine months for a horse to grow a complete new foot and I hoped they wouldn't have to go through discomfort for that long. The cob wasn't pulling me, that was a nice change, and the pony was following on a long lead rein. I promised them some hay, opened the gate and off they went to their new lives.

Had I been a conventional person they would have run across the grass into a field. I haven't mentioned it yet but at this stage in my life I didn't own or rent a field. There were no stables either.

We had a few acres of woodland but less than an acre of it was pasture. It was about a fifteen minute drive from our home in Sussex and I'd decided to winter them there rather than pay a fortune at a livery yard where they would most likely be stabled at night. It wasn't an obvious choice but it had many advantages over the traditional field and stable set up. It didn't get muddy in wet weather and the shelter was excellent. We had to improve the fencing but they seemed amazingly happy there. I had to visit twice a day but I'd have done that anyway at a livery yard unless I paid for extra services.

Our woodland was known as Phie Forest and was used in the Second World War to station a Canadian tank regiment. So instead of lush pasture I was blessed with nettles, brambles, gorse and trees. Most importantly there was the perfect thing to help a horse toughen up his weak and tender feet – concrete.

Road ways, parking areas and the bases of the former accommodation huts abounded amid the trees. On one of the concrete platforms you could see the shape of the shower bases; on another were the remains of the toilets, the plumbing rather than the bit you sit on! The former tank repair shed gave me plenty of storage for hay and could provide stabling in case of illness but I wouldn't bring them in every night in the usual way.

Most horses in Britain, with its wet, soft fields, are brought in at night. Bed time for the horse begins before dark – so three or four o'clock in the afternoon in the winter and he isn't let out again until the morning. Take your horse to a livery yard and that's what you get. A box measuring 12 x12 that becomes a toilet by the morning - smelly places that are damaging for the animal's feet among other things.

The trouble is the horse doesn't appreciate eight hours in bed like us humans. He sleeps for a few minutes at a time preferably with some mates nearby who are standing guard. He's a herd animal who feels safe in a crowd.

Much later, when I had eight of them to look after, I could see how they liked to rest close together. Some will lie down, some will nap standing up and one or two will be awake, fanned out in different directions in case trouble approaches. It's a survival instinct that's worked for them for millions of years.

Sadly, we try to change all that. We isolate them in stables and we stop them moving around. The horse is the most accommodating creature and somehow copes. Sometimes he doesn't and his behaviour and health suffer.

But I've digressed. I didn't want stables for my two and anyway they had a better chance of becoming sound, barefoot horses if they could move all day and night and if their feet were not being damaged by standing in their own urine.

I took the children to the woods that evening to feed the horses. It was such a great place that even my youngest, Max, barely complained that we made this a daily excursion. He was about six at the time; he had a bike and he had a private roadway to ride up and down on.

Tonight was a bit special though. We tied Barnaby up so that Girlie could eat in peace and we put out piles and piles of hay.

'I can't believe they're barefoot,' my daughter, Amber, said, gazing at the new look.

You'd think she'd been waiting a year while I pondered this step. I'd read Dr Strasser's book only a few weeks ago and very little time had been wasted before getting those shoes off.

'We may have to lead them for a while, darling,' I said. 'We may not be able to ride straight away. They've got to get used to it.'

I sighed and set the big boy free once Girlie had finished her bucket. He rushed to the nearest pile of hay with his ears at half mast in case anyone disputed his claim.

'Look at that!' Amber cried. 'He's already running around. He's not bothered. Well done, Barn!'

It was incredible because they seemed perfectly at ease – six hours after having their shoes removed. But we adults know things can go wrong; we know not to count chickens.

Max was making motoring noises but Amber and her mum felt seriously smug. I wasn't going to say anything to detract from that moment as we watched them in their woods.

My set up must have looked odd to outsiders. People would surely think it unkind of me not to give my horses a nice, warm bed for the night. Having a few acres meant we didn't have to deal with outsiders very often! There was no need to explain.

How wrong can you be? You see, we had no water supply. There were no neighbouring houses where I could ask for help but on the east side there was a private hospital. The Horder Centre specialised in hip replacement surgery. It was notable for its success and I could see its tidy grounds and smart buildings when I fed the horses.

I managed without water by bringing it from home using a huge green, plastic water butt which sat on my husband's trailer. It must have been terribly heavy but why worry? No one had to lift it. Turn on the little tap and bingo. Water.

It was great being independent and Phie Forest was very peaceful. The feeling of contentment was to change on day five. The kids had gone off to school, the water butt was filled and off I went with the trailer. There was no hurry, finger tapping a computer could wait and the autumnal views over Ashdown Forest were making claims on my attention.

Then there was an enormous crash behind me and the sound of scraping. My heart leapt into my throat but I couldn't see what was wrong. Had I squashed a deer? What the hell had I driven over? I stopped the car and got out feeling sick, fearing I had caused death and mayhem.

There were pieces of wood spattered across the road and a huge puddle of water. The green butt was leaning at an angle with its bottom on the road. The base had sprouted a massive hole and my precious water was all gone. The butt must have been so heavy it had gone through the floor of the trailer. No one had been injured but I had probably ruined my husband's day; he wouldn't be happy…and it was my fault.

The road was very quiet. No one passed me; no one would help. Strong muscles would have been helpful at this point! I picked up as much of the broken trailer pieces as I could and threw them into the back of the car. The empty butt was now light enough to drag further up the trailer and there was some bailing twine in the boot that would help tie it on board.

It looked a mess but I managed to fix it enough to drive to the woods. Worried that I was arriving with an empty barrel and had water for only one more day, I knew the horses wouldn't be able to stay unless we sorted something out.

Patrick, my husband, took one look at my worried face when I returned and said: 'What's happened?'

'A bit of an accident,' I muttered.

He could see I was fine. The car wasn't battered and he looked puzzled.

'With the trailer. I unhooked it and left it behind. I'm sorry, it's ruined.'

He was emotionless when I told him what had happened. Perhaps he was relieved that I was unhurt. Perhaps he had visions of me lying on the road turned into something yummy for the crows. For once, he wasn't in the middle of a phone call and there was no mobile in his hand.

'Oh, don't worry about the trailer,' he scoffed and then smiled. 'It was pretty old. I'm surprised it's lasted as long as it has.'

'The thing is, I can't stay there unless we get hold of some water. I can't take it up there in buckets.'

'How hard can it be to get water? We'll be fine,' he said, nodding at my lack of faith.

Patrick is tall and well spoken; he's the person to send if your only neighbour is the Queen and you need a cup of sugar. Most of the time he's scruffy though and so he does equally well with travellers and people who eat motorcycle chains to sharpen their teeth.

He phoned the Horder Centre for me. Yes, of course we could use their outside tap. Bring a hose.

That's fine. As much water as you like. Can some of our patients come and watch the horses? That's fine, too. Delighted. New best friends.

'There you go, Chem,' he said, when he came off the phone using my dreadful nickname that needs the flourish of a French accent to make it work. 'You just have to ask. I don't know why you're so shy.'

I'm only shy so he can be arrogant. It seems to work. And he wasn't even upset about the broken trailer.

So, that afternoon, armed with a few reels of hose, I straddled the barbed wire fence between our two properties. The joy of running water. I filled the trough and even had enough to dampen the horses' hay since it was dusty. Meeting Ralph, the grounds man, a few days later was my first chance to find out whether the outside world would think me completely bonkers, or not.

CHAPTER 3

Ralph was a tall man. He had neat, wavy, grey hair that was still as thick as sheep's wool and he was strong from working and cycling. Perhaps he had worked at the Centre for too long because he was fascinated by the arrival of a woman with two horses next door. In the woods! He thought it was bizarre but he was eager to understand and asked questions in a friendly way. He soaked up the answers while the water trough filled and Barnaby and Girlie came for introductions.

In the next few months he became their guardian angel and my greatest supporter. I told him about the barefoot thing and he understood perfectly in a way that non-horsey people do. Without defensiveness.

'Why did people put shoes on them in the first place?' he asked.

It said something about the history of shoes in that vet's book. It was the fault of the upper classes, it seemed.

'Stabling caused the biggest problem for their feet,' I explained. 'It started about a thousand years ago.'

'Really, I had no idea.'

'Knights brought their valuable horses inside the castle walls to keep them safe. Well, they kept them in a stable. But of course that meant they weren't moving around and their feet were standing in wee and poo by the morning.'

'Did that matter?'

'Oh yes, it's the worst thing, it weakens their feet. They start breaking and, I guess, they couldn't manage rough, stony ground. Some blacksmith must have found a way of fixing metal onto them to stop their feet falling apart. It's such a shame because the Greeks had so much knowledge about keeping their feet strong but we seem to have forgotten it. You know, Alexander the Great and his army rode barefoot horses and it didn't seem to slow them down. But then he had a few slaves to tend the animals and stand them in stony streams to toughen them up.'

'You'd think if shoes were so bad for them someone would have complained about it before now,' Ralph said.

'I know. It's so normal for people to shoe their horses but they don't realise the harm it causes. It's not going to be easy getting the horses used to this, though.'

'I can't see little Girlie doing the sort of journeys that Alexander the Great managed,' he laughed. My daughter's pony only reached as high as my tummy. She was a slight, 12.2 hand cutie who didn't know how to snarl. 'You are going to ride them, aren't you?'

'Yep, they're going to be ridden. Very soon. Amber is going crazy. She's very excited about riding a barefoot horse so it will be quite an event.'

'You must be, too, I would imagine.'

'Oh, yes. Of course. Very excited,' I said, quietly. 'And nervous. She's going to be so disappointed if her pony can't manage. Children are not very patient, unfortunately. It's alright for me, I can wait but she won't be happy.'

'Well, horses aren't born with shoes on, are they?' he said. 'They'll be fine; they look comfortable enough and it must save you a fortune. Since you're collecting all that manure up each day, you couldn't let me have some, could you? For the hospital garden.'

It was a fair swap for the water. He must have seen more of the horses than I did for he always told me what they had been getting up to in the morning, whether there had been any fights over a pile of hay, where they went for a kip and how he had seen them playing. He once rang me because he had seen Barnaby rolling around on his back and thought he might be ill. It's one of the signs of colic but you know you are safe when the animal gets up, shakes himself happily and polishes off breakfast in record time.

The boredom that bedevils confined horses was forgotten by those two in the woods. They never ran out of food - thanks to masses of hay - and they always had a few brambles for variety. They could move about, chase each other or have a roll. They were well sheltered and were never cold. But their situation was unusual.

Ralph told me how some visitors to the hospital were shocked by the sight of them.

'Why?' I asked. They weren't thin, they weren't neglected. I even brushed them.

'I know,' he told me. 'I put them right, don't you worry. They wanted to phone the RSPCA but I told them not to bother.'

Oh no, here we go. If they were kept like a car in a garage for twenty four hours a day no one would complain. Believe me, there are plenty of yards that house their horses in a stable for that long. You can see the poor, sad things rocking their heads from side to side. There are even anti-weaving bars to prevent them doing it too much and causing dreadful symptoms from the repetitive motion.

'Why?' I said. 'Just because they live in a wood?'

'They thought they were abandoned. I told them the lady comes up twice a day. They're happy and they're fed, I know that. Don't you worry; I told them.'

Ralph had saved me from an unwelcome visit, not that I had anything to hide but I wanted the horses to be a bit more comfortable before coming under scrutiny.

Within three weeks they were running about the woods and showing little worry over tree roots or fallen branches. The concrete was a different matter. They could walk on it, of course, but it would take them much longer to run across it as if it was grass.

It was time for our first ride. Even I had a childlike excitement at the thought of getting further than the main gate. We would need to ride on the road before reaching the Forest but we could lead them over that bit if necessary.

So no more preparation, no more prevaricating. Amber and I got the horses ready. We tacked them up and we led them over the concrete road to the main gate. So far, so good. I held Girlie while Amber got on.

'OK?' I asked.

'She's fine. Come on, Mum. Hurry up.' She had a grin the size of Christmas even though she was getting big for that pony and her legs were half way to the ground. 'This is going to be so cool.'

I checked the girths, made sure we had our badges displayed to show we had paid to ride on the Forest and double checked to ensure the bridles weren't on upside down. Everything was where it should be except one rider was still on the ground. Finally, I gripped my bottom lip with my teeth, put my foot in the stirrup and swung into the saddle as quickly as I could since Barnaby was notorious for making a quick getaway as soon as he felt my very insignificant weight on his back.

Something was different. Very different. He was standing still.

'He hasn't trotted off,' I called to Amber who was heading for the road. 'This is so strange; it feels weird. He's not the same.'

I don't think she was paying me much attention, she was probably wondering when we'd have our first canter or whether they would be able to gallop yet. She was only ten and might not have appreciated the subtle changes going on.

Subtle!

Who was I kidding? My horse could feel. He was cautious and he was taking every step carefully. He wasn't rushing, that trait would come back to us soon enough, and he didn't really care that a huge lorry had passed by without slowing down. The weird thing was that I could feel what he was feeling. Every stone in the road, the impact of it travelled through his body and into mine. It made me think that shoes had detached both of us from the ground's surface and now we were connected in this strange way.

It felt utterly wonderful. I was riding my horse without metal on his feet. There were no nails and no clattering noise as we walked down the road. We were going for a ride sooner than expected and the joy of it was that he was no longer being harmed. The list of diseases and ailments that Dr Strasser thought were caused by shoeing was as long as the credits for a blockbuster movie. The hoof is not a dead thing at the end of the horse's leg; it's flexible. It supports his heart by pumping blood back around the body; it acts as a shock absorber and takes strain away from tendons and joints. So long as it's a natural, unshod hoof.

For the first time in Barnaby's ridden career his feet were doing what they were designed to do without the interference of a human who thinks he or she knows better. I wished he could tell me what he was feeling. Owners have to interpret the horse's quiet language and it's easy to get it wrong. It's safe to assume he wasn't as elated as me. They are noble, stoic creatures who oblige humans sometimes beyond their own endurance.

Barnaby was doing his best for me and didn't appear unhappy. The only time he's ever bitten me was when I was holding him for the farrier. I'm not making this up, I promise. It must have been an equine protest against shoeing and I owe him an apology for not listening sooner.

If he was suffering without his shoes he knew how to tell me. Although he was an amiable horse, he was perfectly capable of bucking, stopping still, putting his ears back or showing me his temper. His repertoire was vast.

This was our first outing and he seemed to accept this new demand. It was no surprise that he had slowed down. There were two ways of looking at this. Negative – my horse can't cope, he's hurting and won't ever trot on the road again. Positive – every step will make his feet stronger, he's taking responsibility for his own actions and can't afford to spook. He's no longer numb.

'Feels strange, doesn't it, Barn,' I said, patting his neck and trusting him on a long rein.

Even though he was walking slowly we were gaining on a woman who was walking up the lane which had no pavements. Barnaby wasn't silent, his feet made soft, padding noises as opposed to the strike of metal landing like a hammer blow but she didn't hear us until we got to within a metre or two. Uncharitable of me, but I couldn't help smiling when she jumped out of her skin.

We got to the Forest and found to our amazement that we could ride normally. If we picked the right spot they could trot and they could canter. They needed soft grass and preferred even ground. Mud and stones presented a problem – one was slippery and the other hurt so best avoided by finding another route through those trees. It didn't matter to the horse that the path was too narrow or the branches too low. Our legs and our heads didn't come into their thinking so we riders needed to take control to avoid a serious tree bashing.

We didn't know this part of the Forest and picked our way along the top of a huge valley. The top soil was thin, erosion scored deep gullies in the weak grass and straggling birch trees did little to block the distant view. It was magnificent. The colours were from an artist's palette. The bracken appeared like caramel, the pine trees were deep, dark green and the heather was clinging onto its purple with a promise for next year's display. The artist, Monet, should have come here – he didn't need to build a lily garden for inspiration.

Once we had ridden to the end of the track it seemed the only way was down and we let them take their time. It wasn't as slippery as it would get in the winter but it was difficult going until we reached the valley floor where it was grassy, soft and inviting. We gave them their heads and had a good belter, pulling up when we reached the woodland. We were both laughing our heads off because it felt such an achievement. I never dreamed we would be doing this so soon. I had been so worried that Amber would be disappointed but now it felt as though nothing would stop us.

A bit further on was a stream where we let them rest and dip their toes in the water.

'The Greeks used to do this, Amber,' I said. Ralph had been interested and I saw no reason not to bore my daughter with a bit more information. 'Wild horses go to drink from a stream every day and their feet get wet. It's an important part of caring for their feet.'

I might have been droning on or it might have been music to her ears. She rode the pony to the deep part of the stream that Barnaby was avoiding. Girlie was nearly up to her tummy but was splashing about as if this was what life was all about.

'Don't let her fall over in it, darling,' I said, forever worried. 'She's only small, she might drown.'

Amber laughed. 'Wouldn't it be great if we could find somewhere to swim with the horses?'

I was thinking it would be terrible. I had enough trouble controlling my horse when his feet were on the ground. The thought of floating about in a few feet of water was doing something awful to my insides.

'We could go to the beach, Mum. Hire a horse lorry and go for a ride on Camber Sands and then go for a swim. I've heard people do that when it's not busy.'

I saw my get out, coward that I was. 'Sure. If we ever buy a horsebox, we'll do that.'

Fantastic. That was never going to happen. I relaxed and we headed out of the stream, back up the hill to Phie Forest where well-deserved hay and safety were ready to welcome us.

CHAPTER 4

After a few more weeks, being barefoot didn't slow us down. We could go at any pace until we reached stony ground and then Barnaby was looking for alternative routes. He could manage an impressive trot on the roads but slippery ground remained a problem for a long time. Until his feet were working better they had little natural grip and that first winter was like riding a horse on skis.

The pony seemed better on frozen ground than the cob and could still be ridden whatever the weather. Barnaby was having trouble and so I got off and led him home more than once. It was surprising really since Girlie suffered from a painful foot condition when we first had her.

She was a posh girl with Welsh bloodlines and papers to prove it – but, for some reason that I didn't question, was advertised as free to a good home. She had shoes on all four and, without a vet to check her over and no apparent lameness, it was difficult for me to spot that she had a problem.

My farrier saw it straight away. My heart sank when he took me to one side and whispered – 'laminitis.'

It's a nasty condition because the hoof wall begins to separate from the rest of the foot and one of the bones inside can tip and press on the sole. But farriers know their trade and thanks to a careful trim, she remained sound and ridden. I didn't know whether being barefoot would help or hinder a return of the problem especially as I didn't have a trimmer at this stage to advise me.

Those first few weeks after taking their shoes off were a heady mix of excitement and trepidation. We kept a careful watch on their feet but became alarmed. Once we were riding, life was taking a heavy toll on them. An inch of each hoof from the ground was peppered and weakened with nail holes from the repeated fixing of shoes. Once barefoot and ridden, it was almost as if their hooves were disintegrating in front of my eyes. I wished I could phone a friend, a farrier or a vet for advice but knew what their answer would be.

Shoes.

Hiding from the hostile, horsey world was instinctive. Later, it would be possible to face the incredulous and answer their questions with the benefit of experience. But such alarm was needless. The newly-bare hoof usually only crumbles as far as the nail holes – in other words, the first inch from the ground. It looks awful but it grows back very quickly.

That's the thing about barefoot. The hoof is being constantly stimulated by ground contact and grows more rapidly unless you are doing enough riding on abrasive surfaces to give your horse a natural trim. At the beginning this was an impossible goal and very soon their feet would need some attention. It was becoming obvious that I'd have to do it myself and so I bought a rasp and got stuck in.

It's not illegal unless you harm your horse but, let's be honest, there was a distinct possibility of that. Fortunately, my rasp from a budget, mail-order company was a fairly blunt instrument and had little ambition to do much rasping. It was heavy and so were the cob's feet and that is one of the hardest factors to come to terms with. I started giving their hooves a trim each week. My efforts were very tentative. The animals stayed sound, we were riding them and to my inexpert eyes their feet looked…well, OK.

At this stage I was having the occasional nightmare about a nameless farrier who came and put shoes back on the pony. I must have mothered her too much for there was never that worry over the cob.

'Oh, get a life,' my husband said wearily, over a hearty bowl of porridge. 'Why don't you dream about something decent for a change?'

'Like what? No, don't tell me, I can guess. But Patrick, it was so real. The clang of the shoes as she walked. It was horrible. What if they make me go back to that? If there's a complaint against me that could happen, you know.'

'It's not illegal to ride a horse without shoes. Are they limping?'

'No.'

'Are they in pain…or making phone calls to the RSPCA…?'

'Don't joke about that, please.'

'Are they even trying to escape or make pleading eyes at Ralph over the fence?'

'No, they look happy enough and they ride like normal except when I get dragged through the hedgerow. That's a bit annoying.'

'There you go then. Stop worrying.'

'But I'm trimming them myself, with no training and that can't be right. Even I know that. It was bound to be difficult but sometimes it's like I'm the only person in the world doing it. It doesn't matter if people think I'm daft but it's a bit lonely, you know.'

'You're not alone. I think what you're doing is great; I'm proud of you and it's the right thing. Amber thinks so too.'

'I know but if only there was a group of people like me.'

'You better start getting your friends to do the same thing. What about Jeannette?'

'She might be interested. I'll talk to her.'

'And while you're waiting for the rest of the world to catch up why don't you go on a training course with this German vet? One day there will be enough trimmers and you won't have to do it yourself,' he said.

My children were young, it wasn't going to happen. So I ploughed on and then had a stroke of good fortune. Someone recommended a professional trimmer. She wasn't a farrier but she'd trained under Dr Strasser, the vet whose book had set me on this journey. She wasn't near but she was willing to travel two or three hours each way to help my horses.

'I will bring you a professional rasp,' she said on the phone. 'They will need trimming every few weeks unless you are riding them twenty miles a day and I won't be able to come that often.'

'That's fine. I'd like to be able to keep them going between visits.'

Kate was a short but strong woman who was like a breath of fresh air. She arrived at our woods and gave me a broad smile. 'This place is perfect,' she said. 'Look at all this lovely concrete.'

'Wow, really?'

Yes, it was lovely but mainly because we didn't sink into mud and no one could see us. There were long concrete roadways at Phie Forest, from when they drove tanks all over the place, and in the horse's 'paddock' there were a dozen or more platforms where the one-time accommodation huts were. These were now covered in leaf mould about three or four inches thick. Once we had swept some of them clean, they provided the perfect surface to toughen up their feet and put out their hay.

'Ride them on it enough and they won't need much trimming,' said Kate, optimistically. 'If you can't ride them, lead them. Everyone should have this much concrete.'

Autumn was seeping into winter by this time. It was a sharp but dry day and enough leaves had tumbled to the ground to give us plenty of weak sunshine. Kate tied her pale, reddish hair into a pony tail and began trimming away, rasping and paring their feet as if she was fashioning something out of clay. She made it look easy. Eventually, she handed me a rasp and got ready to give me my first lesson. I didn't achieve much but that's probably just as well. The Strasser trim is not easy for the inexperienced.

Kate was a horse owner as well as a trimmer and was competing in some long-distance events – much like a marathon run. Her horse was coping brilliantly although they were often greeted with a few strange looks. Soon, we talked about farriers, stables and shoes and which was the most harmful to the horse. Stabling got my vote since it made the other two necessary.

Kate disagreed. 'Shoes kill some of them, eventually,' she said. 'There's no competition.'

We moved onto farriers. There were good and bad ones, like any profession, but very few, if any, who were offering a service geared towards barefoot ridden horses at that time.

'If only you could get some of them to retrain,' I said.

'It would be perfect, wouldn't it?' she said. 'They already have the skills and they're strong. It's a back breaking job. I got a few threatening phone calls from one of them.'

'Really, what did he say?'

'He was furious. He ranted and raved about me ruining his trade and taking his customers. It was frightening. Hopefully I won't ever meet him face to face. Ridiculous when you think I only have a few clients. It's not as if word has spread rapidly.'

Kate also gave me a sheet of instructions which reiterated the advice in Dr Strasser's book, *A Lifetime of Soundness*. To summarise, it was – keep the horse moving, keep the horse moving...oh, and keep the horse moving. The no-stables rule was not a problem for me but even in a big, open space horses can find time to put their feet up if you present them with a pile of hay. Why bother to walk?

'Spread the hay all over the place; tuck it under some bushes, if you have to. You need to make them work for their supper,' she said. 'Oh, and if they look uncomfortable make sure they keep walking even if you lead them somewhere soft. No standing still.'

The message was loud and clear. We might have talked about abscesses before she left and we needed to again within a few days when Barnaby went sharply lame. My first big hurdle, my first feeling of guilt. At least there was someone to phone. Kate's advice was simple.

'Keep him moving. He'll get rid of it himself if he doesn't stand still.'

The attitude to abscesses was almost to welcome them since they were the horse's way of ridding itself of toxins. My horse was walking as if there was a golf ball in his foot and I was in dire need of my own poison – a double whisky. This was not good.

'Call the vet?' I asked.

'Sure, if you're worried,' she said with amazing sangfroid. 'But try to stop the vet digging into the foot too much. They can drain the abscess but leave you with some awfully big holes.'

Barnaby threw off that uncomplicated but painful lameness without veterinary help remarkably quickly. But over the next few months other styles of trim came to my notice, most of them easier for the owner to maintain between visits. Sometimes the different groups seemed to regard each other with the hostility only known amongst rival religions. Each had its own path to salvation and anyone treading an alternative route was viewed as a misguided sinner.

There were no saints in our woods; my trimming developed its own method but never gained a name! And it seemed to work...not that you should try it at home.

CHAPTER 5

Girlie was a worry. Oh, her feet were fine but she didn't seem right. She wasn't eating much and sometimes her energy was good but at others she was listless. Then there was her weight. She was a bit thin. Could Barnaby be eating all her food? He would have liked to but he was tied up while she got through her twice-a-day bucket. We needed a vet.

I waited for him nervously at the woods, worried that he would confront me about their feet, demand to know who trimmed them or insist the cruelty was ended and they were given shoes to wear. Perhaps, he would treat me like a mother whose urchins had to cook their own dinner and always had snotty noses.

I kept repeating to myself that barefoot wasn't cruel. Shoes were harmful, not me. Saying it enough times gave me strength.

Well, he examined her and checked her teeth but he couldn't find anything wrong. To my surprise, he didn't say anything about them being barefoot. What shocked him was how they were kept.

Yes, they live in a wood.

No, they don't seem to need rugs.

Um…no, we haven't got any stables.

'Well, you've got some grazing, haven't you?' he asked.

'Oh, absolutely. Over there we've got plenty. You just can't see it from here,' I lied, knowing he wouldn't have been impressed with their little bit of open pasture.

For the next few months we pumped food into that pony and kept a careful eye on her. Amber was growing out of her, that much was certain, but there was no way we were going to part with her. She was still the subject of the occasional nightmare and had to stay with me. Friends rode her sometimes and we found a beautiful gelding called Orion that Amber could use.

He was for loan and the owner surprisingly wasn't unhappy with him living in the woods so long as he wore shoes. Girlie came on most of our rides either ridden by one of Amber's friends or I took her on the lead rein rather than leave her behind which she hated. We kept her fit and she seemed to have plenty of energy again but too many bones.

One day, though, we left her behind with some hay. We took Barnaby and Orion for a good ride and when we got back Amber agreed to take Girlie for a walk as she hadn't been out. Off they went – Amber leading her in a head collar while I stayed behind and did some chores. It was almost dark by the time she got back and any mother would have been worried.

'How did you get on?' My voice was a little shrill at the sight of her extremely happy face coming towards me. 'Did she enjoy that?'

'Yeah, she did,' Amber laughed. 'We had a great canter up that really steep hill. You know the one they love.'

Disbelief had me by the throat. 'So, you rode her?'

'Of course. I turned the lead rope into reins and jumped on.'

'With just a head collar? No saddle, no hat?' And it seemed no worries, either.

'Some people I met gave me a funny look. You should have seen their faces. We had such a great time. She loved it; I must do it more often. She's such a good pony and I wasn't too heavy for her. And guess what.'

'What?'

'She didn't buck.'

Laughter got to me. Amber got up to stuff when I wasn't around and most of the time it was fine. This was one of them.

But it was the last time she would ride Girlie who died inexplicably one day when we were on holiday. We never found out what was wrong but she had extremely good feet when she left us. My last memory of her is when a friend came riding with us and Girlie trotted happily on a stony track. She'd made it – barefoot and comfortable.

We were left with Barnaby, Orion and a huge feeling of sadness.

I saw a lot of Ralph, the grounds man, over those winter months. He was lovely to chat to while I was hiding their hay in the bushes and he was curious about our progress. It was easier explaining it all to someone who probably didn't know one end of a horse from the other. He was sympathetic and wanted to learn. He even looked at Barnaby's flexible feet. By this time the crumbling and falling-to-bits stage had stopped, his feet were getting stronger and they were getting bigger.

'Do you see this bit?' I asked Ralph, picking up the cob's foreleg to expose the underside of his foot. 'It's called the frog. It's sort of rubbery and needs to come into contact with the ground but of course it can't if he's wearing metal shoes.' Ralph peered over my shoulder. 'Well, it used to be half this size and it tended to get a bit smelly.'

'I get you,' he said, laughing. 'Fancy a horse having a frog.'

'Funny, isn't it? But watch this.' Barnaby's foot was squeezed between both my hands. 'Can you see that?'

'Blimey, it moves. I never knew hooves could move like that.'

'Exactly. It's only a little bit because it's hard to exert enough pressure but if you squeeze here you can see it. And that's why they should never have a fixed shoe. That's why their feet crack and get ruined by shoeing because the feet spread when the animal lands. If he lands on metal, can you imagine all that jarring? It's terrible for their legs and it ruins their circulation.'

'How come?'

'That veterinary book argues that the foot is an auxiliary pump to the heart and it won't work if it's shod. Simple as that. There you are, Barn,' I said, putting his foot down. 'You are now expected to live forever.'

It was easy to impress Ralph with my new-found knowledge but someone who owned a horse was a challenge and a half. Confidence came with time but the reaction was not always encouraging. Telling a rider that shoes are a terrible thing and might shorten their animal's life is like telling someone *you're cruel, mate*. It doesn't go down well.

It's an accusation they can bat straight back especially if my barefoot horse is tender or not performing as well as theirs. Until Barnaby was out of this awkward transition phase I didn't have much of a leg to stand on. It didn't stop me trying, however. Thoroughbred owners were particularly hostile.

Barnaby is a black and white cob. He's stocky and at 15 hands is not very tall, nothing like a Shire. The correct name for the colour is piebald but some people call them Gypsy cobs because they are much prized by the travelling community. Years before, we used to ride past a yard run by some friendly travellers and they often asked if he was for sale. It must have been his strong, arched neck and his extravagant action.

He looked less impressive in the winter though, so picture me on my long-haired beast with his shaggy mane and mud-stained coat telling the rider of a pristine thoroughbred what they should be doing and why. Put it this way, none of them asked to see Barnaby's frogs. Very disappointing.

Meeting another rider on the Forest, the conversation would go something like this…

Me: (cheerfully) Morning. That's a beauty, fancy a straight swap?

Thoroughbred owner: (tight laughter) Thanks, he is a handsome chap, isn't he? A bit fresh this morning since we can't turn them out thanks to all this awful weather.

Me: (wincing) That's a shame, they love to get out and have a run around and a roll. Mine lives out all the time. I'm doing this natural horse care thing.

Thoroughbred owner: Yes, I can see you are.

Me: It's better for their feet, if they're moving all the time, you see. He's barefoot and it helps him no end not to be standing around.

Thoroughbred owner: Barefoot. How novel. What will they think of next?

Me: Any horse could achieve it, you know. It's not just for the heavier breeds.

Thoroughbred owner: I knew a pony once that didn't have shoes but it was retired, of course. My boy couldn't possibly manage. Thoroughbreds have very weak feet, unfortunately. Well, it was lovely meeting you. How brave you are to go without a stable. (shuddering at the thought.)

CHAPTER 6

It was time to leave the sanctuary of our wood. It was spring. The horses needed more sunshine and the goodness of the grass and my purse needed a break from feeding hay every day. We were offered the use of a small paddock by a friend so we moved home. As many owners will know, spring grass is a potent thing and those two horses had enough native breeding in them to be wild and woolly. They didn't need much food and so of course they got rather fat even though their intake of grass was minimised by using electric fencing. Orion's owner, who ran a riding stables, visited one day and thought her horse was pregnant. Bit of a miracle for a gelding.

'I'm worried about him,' Sonia said, sternly. 'He'll get ill if you carry on giving him that much grass. They don't need it, Linda, they're fat.'

'But what can we do?' They were only on a small part of the paddock and a diet wasn't possible until they'd eaten it down.

'They need a starvation paddock,' she said. 'I couldn't believe it; they look like they're going to give birth. Bring them to my place. Both of them. We've got a bare field that will be perfect.'

'You don't mind if Barnaby comes too? That's very kind of you.'

'They're fat,' she barked. 'Ride them over to me tomorrow. I'll not have you ruining my horse.'

OK – that told me. Even now the embarrassment of that conversation is fresh. I winced and had a complete guilt trip. To be honest, she was right. Native types like Barnaby and Orion would be better off with a handful of gorse instead of the lush grass planted to fatten cows.

Sonia was a very brusque woman but her concern was genuine and it was best that she shared her thoughts. It wasn't easy to hear that I was potentially making two horses ill through my stupid desire to be kind. It was no better than a mother with an overweight child ignoring the warnings of obesity and diabetes.

The guilt was dealt with and replaced with worry. The last place I wanted to be with a barefoot horse was a conventional stable yard. Every other horse and pony would be wearing shoes. They would have all the appearance of being able to walk across anything. Without pain. Because with shoes they were numb and their feet had no ground contact. My horse was doing well but he hadn't toughened up enough to trot down a stony track. He walked across concrete with more care than a shod horse. And he might go lame at any time.

Yes, any horse can go lame but I would be under pressure at the first sign of a limp. If Barnaby was seen to be tender footed, Sonia wouldn't hesitate to tell me to pack it in and call a vet or the farrier. Vets suggest shoes for a lot of foot problems as they instantly make the horse's pain seem to disappear. But shoes don't cure the problem, they only hide it.

Barnaby needed time until his feet acclimatised. He needed gentle riding. His owner needed to hide in the woods. Moving to Sonia's yard meant I was putting myself in the middle of the conventional horse world. Would that world think me cruel? Would someone phone the RSPCA?

I thought about giving up loaning Sonia's pony but then Amber would be without a ride and Barnaby would be on his own – a situation he wouldn't tolerate even if Amber would.

It was a risk but off we went. The horses were turned out in a small field with a few blades of grass. It was barely green and therefore it was perfect. The weight loss was slow, much to my surprise, as I'd expected the lard to fall off them once I saw what they had to live on. Spring grass grows very rapidly and it must have been shooting straight into their hungry mouths as it was almost impossible to see what they were living on.

There were many advantages to having them there. We would have other people to ride with and although we weren't on the Forest, there were some lovely bridle paths. No one seemed to mind that Barnaby didn't have shoes and, although there were a few raised eyebrows, no one challenged me. Why should they? But no one asked me much about it either. Even Sonia wasn't curious and I was loath to repay her hospitality by beating on like a zealot.

We took one very memorable ride together. She was on her beautiful thoroughbred and it was soon obvious that she was a fearless and skilled rider. In spite of Barnaby's bulk, it felt as though I was mounted on a Shetland. If you see a thoroughbred move you will understand. They cover the ground with such grace, their strides are effortless and dear Barn struggled with the speed.

'I thought you were fit,' I told him as we puffed to keep up with the horse in front.

He had his pride and did his best. There was little let up on the stony tracks and although he kept to the edges he had little choice but to plough on or get left behind. It was great fun and during the rare moments when we rode side by side we got into conversation.

Sonia must have seen my horse was under pressure. 'Why don't you put shoes on the fronts?' She wasn't the first person to suggest such a thing. She sounded impatient but at least she wasn't hostile. 'It would make it an awful lot easier for him.'

This was exactly what the farrier had wanted and was an option if you only wanted to do half the job. There was no way I was turning back to horse shoes – not when we had got so far. The progress was invisible to Sonia but I could remember Barnaby's first barefoot steps. He could now walk on rough ground; he couldn't do it at speed but I hoped that would come. It would be useful if it would come in the next five minutes but that wasn't going to happen. My pride was being dented by this conversation - that was all.

We were heading towards home on yet another stony trail. There was grass at the sides and hedges and trees blocking the view of the sweeping hills. It was one of those freezing cold, spring days and my hands regretted that I'd left my gloves behind. Fortunately, we were riding at a cracking pace and generating our own central heating.

Barnaby took matters into his own hands and leapt onto the grass at the side of the track; I was in time to duck the trees while he sampled a few leaves to keep up his strength. I could hear Sonia groaning in dismay.

'Well, the thing is, he will get there,' I called out. My face was down on his neck and branches snapped across my back. I took frequent glimpses to check when I could sit up safely but was in no position to steer him, and me, out of this impasse. 'He's still in the transition period, you see. It might take him a year but I might be lucky as I think he's making...' more ducking... 'very good progress.' Finally we left the bushes and the cob had the evidence of a pretty good meal dangling from his mouth. 'I just have to ride him with a little consideration, that's all.'

Sonia turned to me from the superior height of her spirited, bay gelding. 'Consideration?' she said. 'That's one word that is not in my vocabulary.'

She trotted off and we shuffled behind. I might laugh about this now...but not then. Even to my own ears I sounded a bit daft.

Had I ridden on my own, I would never have taken him at such speed on the rough tracks. I might even have got off and led him but pride does awful things to people and I was not immune to the desire to show that my horse could manage without shoes; he could keep up.

If he was going to get an abscess while we were at Sonia's this would have been the time. I checked his feet over the next few days. There was some bruising on his soles, so I gave him some arnica and held my breath. He was promised extra carrots if he remained sound. It must have done the trick because he didn't let me down.

Looking back at that period, I did well to get through it without any repercussions. Kate visited once while we were there to give Barnaby a trim and check on our progress. She was pleased and encouraging but I could tell she felt for me in my changed situation. I tried to hide from the other owners that I was trimming him myself between visits but the threat of the raised eyebrows was very real if anything went wrong.

CHAPTER 7

It's possible that people thought me a little obsessive because I tended to talk about barefoot horses rather a lot. Thankfully, there were some converts. Dr Strasser's book did the rounds of my friends and some came to see Barnaby and his new look for themselves. If only he could march over stony ground like it was grass but it was still early days. He hadn't gone lame and for that he had my eternal gratitude. I began to relax.

Sonia and I developed a strange but awkward friendship in which we reached an unspoken agreement not to mention *the issue*. We got on pretty well considering we came from different planets. It was OK...or so I thought.

There was one great advantage in being at her place and that was holiday cover. The nightmares about an uninvited farrier doing the evil deed while my back was turned abated and Sonia had a list of instructions to make sure my cob was happy. His feet were given a little rasp in the field and he was warned to behave himself.

Did he? Apparently not. He wasn't a horse that liked to be left on his own and Sonia had asked me if they might ride Orion while we were away.

'Of course,' I said. 'He's your horse, after all. I'll leave his tack here for you. Make sure you stick another horse in with Barnaby though. He goes nuts and brings down fences if he thinks he's abandoned. And whatever you do, don't put him on his own in the stables.' I was laughing at this point as I recounted the time he got himself over a stable door to escape loneliness in the early days of our friendship. 'It's funny; he wreaks havoc but never seems to get injured.'

Sonia promised she would take care but she must have thought I'd been joking because she didn't take me seriously. She thought I wasn't tough enough on my animals; they probably needed a firmer hand. What nonsense to say he couldn't be on his own, etc, etc.

On my return we heard that he'd disappointed his carer. There had come a day when all the ponies on the yard were needed for a ride and Barnaby was left alone in a well-fenced field. He didn't escape. There you go, I was wrong. But as soon as company returned he dashed out of the enclosure and made a bid for freedom with a huge buck.

'He's extremely naughty,' Sonia complained. 'It wasn't about being lonely at all. Oh, I know you love him but he's a pain. And another thing...'

'What? You didn't put him in a stable, did you?'

'No, I didn't dare. I didn't want my stables smashed to bits by your dreadful animal. I'm worried about Orion.'

'What about him? He's OK, isn't he?'

'No, he's not. He was refusing his jumps. Terrible. He's gone to my friends for retraining. You're not strict enough with him and he's taking advantage of you. He's got enormous scope. She got him jumping three foot fences and he could easily do more in the right hands.'

It seemed that our hands were not the right ones. She was probably right. She was seriously displeased with me and there wasn't much to say. Orion was her pony and we were letting him go downhill.

Barnaby was a pain and sadly Sonia was not enamoured of his gentle and loving nature. She hadn't seen the way he checks out your shoes to see if you were going to ride him or not, that was always an endearing trait but I thought it was too late to get him to perform.

Amber took the loss of her loan pony surprisingly well. That's the thing with loaning a ride – you never quite feel they are yours. They might go back to their owner as this one had so you don't give them the same emotional commitment no matter how well you try to care for them. She didn't cry but she must have had some feeling of humiliation or annoyance unless I lied sufficiently well at the time to protect her from it. Well within my scope. It was time to organise my departure.

I phoned my friend Bev who used to give me riding lessons. 'You don't know of a companion horse, do you? Barnaby needs a friend.'

My situation was uncomfortable rather than desperate but I probably would have taken anything. An unrideable horse needing a quiet life or a retirement home would have been ideal. Respite was needed until I could find something else for Amber to ride.

'Well, I might know of one that could still do a bit of riding. I'll phone you back,' she said.

Enter Shanty.

We went to visit this shaggy pony thought to be in his twenties. That's pretty old but he still had a bit of get-up-and-go. He needed to live out thanks a respiratory problem, called COPD, which meant he was highly sensitive to dust. Perfect, he wouldn't get a stable with us. And although he could still be ridden he didn't like working in a schooling arena. Extra perfect, we didn't have one of those. The little girl who owned him had graduated to a bigger and more youthful ride and they couldn't afford to keep two.

At 13.2 hands, he was bigger and stockier than Girlie. He had a large head, pink-rimmed eyes and a pink nose as if he had drunk too much red wine. We called him The Pink Pony and gladly took possession with promises to care for him forever. They knew I meant it but the little girl's eyes were streaming with tears when we turned up with a trailer to take him to his new life.

It was a relief to be my own boss again. No one was looking at me with strange, disapproving looks and no one was going to suggest a return to metal shoeing. I was free to get on with the job I'd started less than a year ago – to produce a sound, barefoot ridden horse. Barnaby was nearly there but what would this new boy bring?

So far we had taken two horses through the transition to barefoot. Girlie, in spite of her laminitic history, had been easier than Barn who was still prone to slipping and avoided stones. The ease with which Shanty took to life on his own feet left me open mouthed. Unbelievable. For a few days, it seemed unreal.

He came with shoes on but his previous owners were quite happy for him to have them off. So, a farrier was called, a different one.

He came in a little white van with the usual gas forge in the back. He'd been booked to remove the shoes from a retired pony and didn't quibble.

'Want them off, do you?' he said, double checking.

'Yes, he's a companion. Not ridden.'

It's quite usual, even in conventional circles, to remove shoes from a retired horse so the request wasn't wacky. He gave Shanty a little trim in exchange for twenty pounds.

How easy was that? The job was achieved with no acrimonious words, no throwing of tools and the usual exchange of horse stories and gossip.

The horses were staying at a field offered to me by my friend, Anette, who wanted to get a horse of her own but hadn't got round to it yet. That first ride was a revelation. Shanty had strong feet that were beautifully concave and showed no damage from years of shoeing. It was as if he didn't notice the difference.

We had to ride up a stony, unmade road before we got to the Forest – a route that would take us over the much-photographed Pooh Bridge. Yes, the one made famous by A.A. Milne. The place where Piglet and Pooh threw sticks into the stream from the bridge and then ran to the other side to see whose came through first. It was not the sort of ride you might choose for an animal that has only had his shoes off for a day but there was no other route.

Amber might have needed to lead him but Shanty didn't miss a beat. 'I don't believe it!' I said. 'He must be numb.'

'He feels fine,' Amber said. 'He's really nice. He's enjoying himself.'

The pony didn't try to get off the stones once even though there were verges available had he been in pain. He simply marched.

Pooh Bridge was surrounded by tourists, taking pictures and playing Pooh sticks and Shanty didn't bat an eyelid – the joy of an experienced horse. Some Japanese visitors turned to us and snapped away. With his big head and mournful eyes, Shanty could have passed for Eeyore.

'He's not numb at all, Mum,' Amber said, once the bridge was behind us. 'He's simply got really good feet. Do you think we'll be able to have a canter up that hill?'

'Why not? If he can do it. He's very sensible, isn't he? He won't be the fastest horse and you won't be able to jump him but it looks like he's going to give you a nice ride. I can't believe his feet. It's not fair.'

'I guess they can't all be difficult. Perhaps it's time we had an easy one. Come on, Mum, keep up.'

We rode through the woods, past some fabulous houses that nestled on the edge of the Forest and soon reached one of the firebreaks that lend themselves to riders wanting a faster pace. There were the usual signs of erosion but some nice, flat grassy bits for us to have a run. Amber tried Shanty up the hill on his newly bare feet. He took his time as he had given up his racing days and let Barnaby go in front.

We slowed at the top of the hill and I turned to my daughter, laughing and relaxed. 'He doesn't want to retire, does he? What a lovely boy. Shanty, you can stay. For as long as you like.'

I wanted to hug Amber but the horses were in the way. It was such a milestone. We'd actually done it. Two comfortable animals without shoes. Without pain. Without harm. Yes!

CHAPTER 8

Over the next couple of years we gained another two horses giving the impression we were growing our own herd. Amber got a pony that she could jump – not that we were going to shows – but there were logs on the Forest and she was full of ambition. Cloud fitted the bill and hardly dented the pocket thanks to her seventeen years and complete lack of marbles.

She was once quite a posh lady with Arab in her blood, legs that could do fancy dressage moves and a history in the showing world. Showing is a strange horse discipline - a little like Crufts - where the horse has to move and behave beautifully and is best owned by a good hairdresser. Sorry, but it's dreadfully boring.

We went to visit Cloud before buying but more and more problems were slowly revealed. This horse was terribly nervous of stables. She had a fall in one and now wouldn't step inside the door. That wouldn't be a problem. More seriously, a rider couldn't get on her by putting a foot in the stirrup. Oops.

Her sellers said the previous owners to them had a unique method of getting on which involved cantering her in a circle and running alongside her, giving the rider a leg up on the move. It sounded lethal. We didn't try it.

They had done a lot of work with this nervous mare and had calmed her sufficiently to get on with a stationary leg up once she had been warmed up by running around for twenty minutes on a long lunge line.

Amber, who was keen to try her over some jumps, eventually got on and they looked stunning together. The animal's paces were fluid and those dressage moves were impressive. After a while, Amber rode her towards a small jump but it wasn't the pony's strength and she turned into a shape like a banana. The rider fell off.

I must have felt sorry for Cloud as we bought her the next day. My poor daughter. I should apologise to her. No expense spared, my darling.

Thankfully children bounce and they don't care. They have fun, they go too fast and they jump logs that are enormous. They also hide on their horse in the trees and pounce on their mother when she's riding along in a dream and not paying much attention. That paid me back, I suppose. Amber had fun with that pony; she even went to shows and won a few rosettes jumping thanks to an adorable neighbour with a horse box and an ambitious daughter.

Cloud came to us with bare feet since she'd been a brood mare due to those fancy bloodlines of hers. So, once again we had an easy time on the foot front and my trimming wasn't being challenged. My skills were improving and I continued my one-to-one training with Kate and another trimmer who lived nearer.

'It would be wonderful to find a horse that has problem feet, wouldn't it, Mum,' Amber said on one of our rides. 'Then we can prove that it works.'

'Yes, it would. It might be a lot of work but it would be worth it. So many of them are put down when they are young but people don't realise they might get better if they weren't wearing shoes.'

'Surely, we could find something. I could take it for walks until it got better. I'd help you.'

By this time we had bought a house with some grazing and scoured the Friday Ad over the next few weeks. I even phoned one advertiser who was looking to rehome a mare that suffered from a lameness called navicular which gives them pain in the heel area. Dr Strasser was adamant that it was a man-made problem caused by the impact of shoeing. The healing process might be long-winded depending on the damage but Kate assured me that the chances were good once you restored what they called hoof mechanism. Basically, it means the ability of the hoof to move naturally.

I explained how hopeful I was to the poor woman with the mare. She was horrified.

'Take the shoes off?' she cried.

'Yes, they're very damaging. They could even be the cause,' I said.

'Don't you realise she would be even worse? She wouldn't be able to walk without her shoes. It would cripple her.'

'Not for long. The thing is...'

This telephone conversation was not for long either. I can't remember if she put the phone down on me but she might as well have. I didn't get anywhere with her. I felt for the poor animal but was powerless to help and let it go.

My husband, surprisingly, was supportive of my attempts to give myself even more work with horses. It might have been the prospect of getting a horse without paying for one. He had such confidence that my regime would cure the horse so he must have been as daft as me since I was still relatively inexperienced in spite of all the coaching. He and Amber would scour the ads between them, finding possible contenders and making me phone up about the sick or unwanted.

'Don't bother telling them what you plan to do,' he said. 'You're frightening them. They don't understand.'

He could sometimes be irritable about the time I spent with the horses rather than doing the year-end accounts but at others he was my greatest supporter, challenging other horse riders we met in a way that I was fast becoming tired of. Amber agreed with him.

'No, don't say anything. You've got to think about the poor horse, Mum. These people can't possibly know what's wrong with horse shoes if vets don't even understand it.'

She was right. I had yet to hear of a sympathetic vet and it seemed our medical profession was still immune to the possibility that barefoot could help to heal horses. They should have been at the forefront of this movement but were notable for their absence.

There was an increasing number of people, women mostly, who were qualifying as barefoot horse trimmers and not just from the Strasser stable. There was also an American farrier called Jaime Jackson who had turned his back on the trade and set up a training programme for trimmers after studying the wild horses in the United States.

As it happened, I didn't have to lie or make a phone call to get myself another horse. My friend, Anette, was in a spot of bother. She had bought her dream horse and all was going well until she decided to get the mare some company and took on a loan horse. Her mare was a huge, warm-blood type but she was being beaten up by the newcomer. It happens sometimes when you introduce field companions for the first time but Anette wasn't happy and she wasn't keeping the *friend*.

'I've had the vet up to my horse, she's very badly hurt. The new one is such a bully. I don't trust it any more.'

'What made you get it?' I asked.

'Liquorice was lonely and now I'll be getting a huge vet's bill. I've told the owner but she won't pay it.'

'What's it like?'

'It's got something wrong with its feet. I can't remember what.'

'Laminitis?'

'No, I don't think so. It began with *n* but she's not lame and she came with a sack load of Bute. We were going to ride her but we've never had the chance.'

Bute is an anti-inflammatory commonly used on horses in pain.

'Navicular?'

'That's it. We haven't had to use the painkillers. Anyway, I told the woman I can't keep it any more. You won't believe what she said. She can't afford to keep it so she'll have it put down. Shot.'

Air whooshed into my lungs. 'Don't let her do that. How horrible. What about the rescue centres?'

'They're full and they're not interested. They're overloaded with work.'

'No, I'll take it. Don't worry, it will be alright. We mustn't let that happen, perhaps I can talk to the owner.'

'Will you really take it? That would be great. When do you want to come and see it?'

'I'll come tomorrow. By the way, what is this horse?'

I had no idea whether I was taking on a Shetland or a Shire, although I thought the latter was unlikely. I only knew it had the heel pain caused by navicular – always be careful what you wish for.

'It's a thoroughbred mare,' Anette told me. 'She's about 15.3 and she's called Carrie.'

Amber's eyes lit up when she heard. 'When can we go and see her? I'll try her out. We'll soon get her better and she won't be able to bully Barnaby.'

Carrie was a beautiful, bay mare and appeared laid back and calm when we met her. She didn't seem in pain and walked fine but her feet were a basket case. I have never seen anything like them in my life. They were like Aladdin's slippers - long and curling upwards. She had shoes on but it was a shock that anyone could have let her feet get so out of shape.

'When was she last shod?' I asked Anette.

'I don't know. Do they look bad?'

'Terrible.'

'Apparently, she's always had trouble keeping the shoes on. These are nailed and glued to her feet.'

I stared at the poor mare and winced. The task was terrifying but I couldn't leave her. She didn't have long. There was a bullet out there waiting to get her. Not because she was sick but because her feet, in shoes, had got so bad that she was nearing the end of her life. Professional help was essential.

'Can you have her reshod before she comes to me? This is too much for me to handle.'

'Sure, I'll get my farrier to do it.'

'But we'll need the shoes off the backs. If she wants to do some kicking she can do it without the weaponry.'

Amber tried Carrie in a sand school. Walk and trot were straightforward. Canter was a perpetual stream of bucks. Pain was a possibility. Brilliant! Another fine acquisition. Watch out for the headlines – Daughter Sues Mother over Cheap Horse Scandal.

It was easier to persuade Carrie's owner that she should come to me. She was sceptical about the horse's chances of being barefoot and comfortable but relaxed when I explained that if she wasn't sound we wouldn't ride her.

'I won't put your horse on Bute so she can be ridden. We've both got our own horses, you know, I'm not doing it for that reason. It would be awful to put her down, that's all; she's got years in front of her. If she's not rideable she can still have a home here.'

Carrie's owner nurtured some other doubts. 'She's not a novice ride. She's an ex-eventer but started refusing jumps probably when she got navicular. I got her after that. You shouldn't really put your daughter on her.'

'Oh, don't worry about Amber. She's a better rider than me.'

I didn't say, she's young and she bounces but I did give an assurance that Carrie could come here with her front shoes on and then we would assess what to do for her.

So, Carrie came and was turned out with the others in a large field so there was plenty of room to sort out the hierarchy. The next day from the kitchen window, you could see Barnaby's white hair flying in little tufts in the air and there was the sound of squealing. We rushed outside but they'd stopped. Carrie wasn't a bully…but she was already the boss. Barnaby must have been the only one to give her a verbal challenge but he didn't keep up the fight. She didn't touch the ponies and Cloud seemed to adore her.

As expected, Carrie's feet were the biggest issue. Anette's farrier had put on a new set of front shoes but it didn't look as though he had trimmed her feet. I couldn't blame him since they were quite a mess. My friend, Roseanna, who collected the mare in her trailer with me, looked at her feet in shock.

'How could anyone let them get that bad?' she said. 'What was the farrier thinking of? Perhaps you should wait until the ground is softer before you take her shoes off, Linda. It's going to be tough for her.'

It was a good idea. If only nature had allowed it. Without the glue, Carrie's shoes fell off within ten days. One at a time. I was busy trying to find someone to take off the second when it followed the first.

Carrie was barefoot.

CHAPTER 9

The ground was hard and her feet exploded. They cracked and took on the appearance of drift wood. It was a mystery how she managed to walk on them but horses get used to discomfort and Carrie must have been a trooper. We didn't ride her while they looked like this but she ran around the field as if nothing was much wrong. It was a dry summer and the ground was as hard as concrete. Once again we were without some of the conventional facilities – no stables – but there was something that Carrie really appreciated. A foot bath.

It was built out of railway sleepers, pond liner and carpet. The carpet stopped their feet piercing the pond liner and we filled it with enough water to cover their hooves. It stood at the top end of one of the fields and in hot, dry weather they went there in turn for their breakfast. Carrie took to staying in the water. It must have soothed her feet and her hay was put on the edge so she could linger for longer.

The aim was to mimic the daily routine of wild horses who drank from streams and thereby got their feet wet. Domesticated horses rarely got the chance but it was thought to be an important element of their foot care. The footbath became Carrie's place for a snooze. It helped to rehydrate her feet but did little to change their appearance. They remained an embarrassing reminder of the struggle she faced.

At least we could call help. My trimmer, Kate, seemed unfazed and said she had seen worse. She trimmed Carrie and told us to keep her moving. Walk her; ride her if she could do it.

There's a lovely story in Dr Strasser's book about a man in Australia whose horse was incurably lame. The vets had given up on it and advised euthanasia but the owner was in despair and couldn't bring himself to do the deed. So he did something that we can't do in England. He took the horse into the outback and set him free amongst the wild herds.

Well, obviously he had no idea how the animal would fare or whether he would be accepted by his wild cousins. Perhaps the dingoes would intervene and turn him into lunch but the owner spotted the horse a couple of years later when he was driving through the outback.

It was his horse; there was no mistaking it thanks to the unusual markings. And he was sound. He was cured of a lameness that had stumped the professionals. He'd achieved this without drugs and without an operation. Movement had been the healer.

I looked at Carrie's rotten feet and wondered whether she could be ridden towards a cure. I couldn't set her free but knew there had to be a solution if her lifestyle was natural enough and she clocked up enough mileage. That story gave me hope.

She got through that hot, dry summer and became rideable. In winter, she made some significant improvement. The wet gave her feet constant rehydration and the soft ground allowed her to be comfortable. Her feet were flat though and slipped in the mud. Stony ground troubled her.

We shared her riding but she was more Amber's horse thanks to her tendency to travel from 0 to 60 mph in ten seconds. Her style made us wonder whether she had raced, there seemed to be a deep memory of starting gates inside her and you had to make sure your weight was forward enough for takeoff with every canter. Stopping had its own challenge since requests were ignored, or at best, discussed with an animal who had the bit between her teeth.

She was a very talented jumper and, with the right ground, she did a bit of cross country training with Amber. Her owner had told me she had evented but began to refuse jumps, presumably due to pain, and was retired from competition. So, we trusted her to do the same at this lower level if anything troubled her.

That's one of the wonderful things about riding a barefoot horse. You can feel instantly if there are problems. The impact of every stone and every tree root travels through their body and yours and you know if it hurts them or not. They are wise creatures. If they hurt, they slow down. If the road is too hard, they get to the verge. If the jump is too much, they stop. The owner of a barefoot horse is so in touch with her horse's feet that she rarely makes demands that are too great.

It is so easy to do with a shod horse. How many riders have asked their horse for a fast trot up the road? The horse can do it so why not?

The vibration caused by that shoe landing on the road travels up the animal's leg at a frequency that is said to be damaging to living tissue. But the horse gets no warning of the danger; he can't feel his feet, remember? So, off he trots. He's on a track now away from the cars. His owner thinks a canter would be nice. He's happy to oblige. The soles of his feet aren't touching the ground but that doesn't mean the ground is having no impact. It is. He can't gauge the unevenness of the track, the shoe is spreading the contact pressure of the stones evenly along its surface. But the vibration is increasing.

He is wearing nailed-on metal which has been fixed to his foot while it was raised off the ground. Think about it; the foot spreads when it lands on the ground if it is bare and it is at its narrowest when lifted...and shod. That horse is wearing shoes that are tight and jarring.

The scenario I'm describing is thought to be the cause of a lot of arthritis as well as concussive laminitis, an inflammation from riding on hard ground. I'm not saying barefoot horses don't suffer such things but they are less likely to be caused by a rider asking for too much.

Carrie walked onto our neighbour's lorry that day very happily so that our two girls and their horses could visit a cross country course that was for hire a few miles away. Her feet had lost their look of driftwood but they were still unimpressive. I wasn't sure if she would cope but knew Amber would put a stop to anything that would hurt her.

The jumps were natural and solid. They were in large fields and my neighbour, Caroline, and I followed as they went round the course. The further they went, the bigger the jumps became. Both horses were excited but everyone was having fun.

If the ground was stony, either on the approach or on the landing, Carrie was excused. There was no way we could chance her on unsuitable surfaces. I have a very happy memory of her leaping over an obstacle and landing in a small lake as though it was the easiest thing in the world. Oh, yes, the Olympics, here we come! Well, Amber had wanted to try swimming with a horse.

We didn't go back to square one in the spring but Carrie's feet began to deteriorate again. The dry weather didn't help and, although she spent time in the footbath, there were new cracks appearing in her feet. There were times when she was uncomfortable and it was disappointing that she wasn't *cured* after nine months of being barefoot. She was a worry but she was rideable and we carried on whenever she could.

Once again, it was good that we lived in an isolated spot. My neighbours rode with me, they were mildly interested in what I was doing but they weren't rushing to follow in my footsteps. Polite people. Having my own place meant I didn't have to field hostility. But it was out there and I had to heed its warnings.

It reached me via a copy of Horse & Hound given to me by another neighbour. A prosecution for cruelty against a barefoot trimmer. I was shocked by the report.

Jo Kowlenski had been found guilty of cruelty towards a pony with laminitis – one she had been trying to save. It was one of the worst things that could happen and made me feel instantly sick. To be accused of cruelty. To an animal. Give me an accusation of drug taking or murder any day. I wanted to send her messages of support but didn't know how. I spoke to Kate who was also shaken but not quite so stirred.

'She isn't the only one,' she told me. 'A livery owner has also been prosecuted.'

'Why?'

'For keeping a barefoot horse that was badly lame.'

Metal horse shoes were walking over my grave. They were knocking on my door, keeping me awake.

'I don't understand,' I wailed. 'Can't they see these people are trying to help horses that everyone else has given up on? How can they say it's cruel? Go to some livery yards and see the poor animals shut in a stable for 24 hours a day. That's cruel. Horse shoes are cruel. Injuring and deforming their feet. Why doesn't the RSPCA do something about that?'

'Unfortunately, they don't agree with us.'

'Well, they're blind.'

Kate didn't share my aggressive stance. She was calm and steady and wanted to reach out to the conventional horse world and the veterinary profession in a rational way - convince rather than hit over the head. It was a much more comfortable approach since she was in the front line. She was trimming horses in livery yards, meeting farriers who frowned at her but snarled less and less. The hostility was washing over her and she was hoping to make an impact by doing a good job, helping horses to walk on their own feet once more.

My shoulders sagged. We were David against Goliath. No, we weren't so well matched. We were a bunch of women, mainly. Some had become trimmers, some were owners of mostly non-competition horses and there still weren't many of us. There was one vet from Germany who had written a couple of fascinating but controversial books on keeping barefoot horses – but very few converts.

Here we were, trying to influence a world that nailed shoes onto race horses while they were still babies, before their feet were fully grown. Virtually every competition horse in the land wore metal and nearly every happy hacker. It was so universal that very few owners or professionals got to see a healthy natural hoof. They didn't know how much it expanded once free of the shoe, how the hoof wall thickened or how the frog grew in size over time.

Didn't they realise how the horse's foot moved if you squeezed it hard? Vets were scientists. Surely, they knew all this and so how could they advise nailing an inflexible metal shoe onto a moving part of the horse? Advise it they did for the good of the horse who they were convinced couldn't manage to work without them. They were still suspicious and hostile to the alternative we were suggesting.

Dr Strasser spoke at Jo Kowlenski's trial but failed to influence the verdict. The pony had been in last-chance saloon and Jo had taken it on from the owner in an attempt to save its life. She was a newly qualified trimmer and had done her best for the animal. It was badly lame but she was hoping that trimming and time would make some difference.

Perhaps it would have. Who knows? The RSPCA intervened before she could find out and argued that she had added to the pony's distress. It's not illegal to trim a horse's feet but you are not allowed to fit a set of shoes unless you are a qualified farrier. You are not allowed to harm it either. Some might argue that the law protects the farriery business more than it protects horses from cruelty but you'd never hear me sticking my neck out like that.

Such a liar. I'll stick my neck where I please. The RSPCA does some brilliant work but is very entrenched in the traditional horse-care model. We've been brought up believing the RSPCA will protect animals from harm, from cruelty, but this case showed me the organisation in a very different light.

The charity says it rarely prosecutes as it prefers to advise and educate. If so, it would do well to educate itself about the harm caused by shoes.

The prosecution in the Kowlenski case argued that the pony was suffering and the court agreed. Yet there was a greater criminal at work in all this. Horse shoes. Someone, or something, made that pony lame with laminitis before Kowlenski took it on. But none of the professionals who cared for the pony before her were made to account for their actions. No one was prosecuted for nailing metal onto its feet and causing the problem in the first place. I couldn't understand why the traditionalists still didn't get it.

The court case made me examine my conscience and made me think carefully about each of my four horses who were working barefoot. Let me give you an update on their progress.

Shanty – goodness, I didn't have to worry about The Pink Pony. He was as old as the hills. His feet never cracked, they were beautifully concave and he could still happily do a two-hour hack on the Forest. He made my heart sing every time he took a new child for a ride. I could trust him with a baby on his back, we used him for kid's birthday parties and he even took me a few times when Barn wasn't well. He'd spent his life in shoes and lived to tell the tale. He made me so proud.

Cloud – my daughter's 14.2 pony who had left behind a boring showing career, was as mad as a hatter but occasionally kept her head together enough to jump clear at local shows. Her feet were solid and didn't have a crack or a chip. Amber took her cross country training once with our neighbour and I remember Cloud tackling a large obstacle and landing in a dry, stony river bed.

Don't forget all the impact of landing was on one foot. There was no flinch and no pause. She'd come to us barefoot but with feet a bit ragged and over grown. She'd had an abscess once but had marched it out within two days. Cloud was absolutely fine. We felt like putting a neon sign on her every time she went to a show just so that other riders would notice her outstanding brilliance.

Barnaby - my black and white cob, whose feet had cracked and shown signs of strain while he was still shod, had struggled during his transition to barefoot with slipping and would avoid stony tracks even if it meant knocking my head off with tree branches. He was winning the battle at last. He could trot on the concrete road to our house and keep up in canter on ground that he would once have steered clear of.

I rode him with my neighbour, Caroline, who suggested putting the speed up on a rough track. It occurred to me that she was setting me a test but he cantered happily while her dog ran beside us, heading for home. The crack on his nearside hind hoof had shrunk but hadn't disappeared. Farriers had complained that his white feet were weak but now they were as tough as nails and his speed never altered on rough terrain. Yes, Barn was a very good barefoot ambassador. It hadn't been quick but I was overjoyed that he had finally made it.

Carrie. Oh, dear. Carrie remained a worry. Her feet were bedevilled by cracks and they were flat and small. Her hinds were showing signs of lasting improvement but the fronts were letting us down.

I was trying vitamin and mineral supplements, foot baths and regular trimming. She was ridden but we were careful with her on rough ground. She was careful with herself. She looked fantastically well and was the fastest horse we had. What a great ride! But those feet...

I talked to my husband about my worst fears. 'What if they take her away?'

'They're not going to see her,' he reasoned.

We were clearing up after dinner. Well, I was and he wasn't giving me his full attention. He didn't realise how nervous I was about all this; didn't know how it could go so horribly wrong. He might have to stand by me while I battled with an accusation of cruelty. At least my kids were young and would save me from a spell in prison.

I made him put down his paper and look at the Horse & Hound. 'Read it,' I said. 'That poor woman now has a criminal record. I'm doing the same as her.'

After a few minutes he let out a breath, stood up and walked towards me. He put his arms around me and I started crying. Crying for that poor woman, the poor pony and all the animals who were suffering in horse shoes including the one I saw once in Spain who was resting its feet, one after the other. On and on. It must have been suffering from laminitis but I couldn't take it home with me. There were so many I would never be able to help.

Because the world wasn't listening. And even when it listened, it didn't believe. I cried because I was frightened. I was frightened about losing Carrie. I would have to stand back and watch as they took her away from me, saying I was cruel to her. And if they took her away – they would have her put down. I was her only hope but I simply wasn't brave enough to do this any more. The fight in me was looking defeat in the eye. I was a law abiding, middle class woman having a mild panic attack.

'What if I'm reported, Patrick? What if the RSPCA see her? Everyone around here knows I'm trimming her myself; I make no secret of it. Oh, God, they might take me away from you!'

'Who's going to report you, Chem?' he said, rubbing my back. 'No one around here thinks you are cruel. Our neighbours are lovely and they've seen how much she has improved. Don't be silly. You're doing a brilliant job.'

'Have you seen Carrie's feet?'

'Yes, they're better than they were. Thank God, you've got photos of how they used to be. I really don't think you have to worry. How was your ride today?'

'Oh, she went like the clappers again. I went to that spot she loves where she really takes off,' I said, sniffing and laughing. 'She was fine and she trotted on the road for a bit. I gave her feet a bit of a rasp but they still look a mess.'

'They look like they need a bit of engine oil. Why don't you oil them?'

He gave me some tissue to stem the flow. 'Well, I'm not meant to. Wild horses don't use it, do they? She's not a Morris Minor, you know.'

'Stick some oil on her feet. It might help. And then I think I'd better take you to the pub. She needs some oil and you need a double whisky. I don't want you losing sleep over this.'

Sadly, conversations like this were repeated on a regular basis. I don't know how Patrick put up with me and my paranoia. I still suffered the occasional nightmare about a farrier who was coming to nail shoes onto Girlie's feet - even though she had been dead quite a while. Oh, dear...

CHAPTER 10

My trim was gaining in confidence. It was still supervised; it needed to be as Carrie's feet were so troublesome.

The internet provided a window to the outside world. Until this moment, there had only been me and a few local converts plus my trimmer to give a sense of community. With a few taps on the keyboard there was access to the rest of the world, to places where suspicion was being overcome.

There was a mounted police force in the USA which was converting to barefoot. Unbelievable. I read it again and again. One of the police officers had qualified as a trimmer and the animals were now pounding the streets on their own feet.

Next came news of a race horse trainer in the UK who was producing winners who had no metal on their feet. The racing industry isn't known for its radical approach – what a rebel! I'd always wondered if someone would discover the superiority of barefoot and now, it seemed, someone had.

The story of one horse in particular was especially inspiring. Saucy Night was the first barefoot horse to win a race but the interesting thing was that he'd been an utter failure until then. He had never overtaken another horse in his entire career. Simon Earle, the trainer, took him on as a break down – in other words, he wasn't well. He had been thin and his tendons were damaged; his feet were a mess.

He was allowed to rest, he was kept barefoot and he regained his weight and strength. Training restarted and he was a different horse. He was a winner.

Then there were the livery yards. News reached me of people who were setting up specialist yards for barefoot animals. There were only a few but some were going into business rehabilitating those who were struggling with the transition to barefoot. Wow!

But let's not forget the long-distance riders. A significant number were succeeding in competitions with barefoot horses and manufacturers were making better and better hoof boots to replace conventional shoes and help with the transition. While I had been battling with fears and doubts about Carrie's feet the world had moved on. It was time to catch up.

I took a deep breath. I took stock. It occurred to me that if a nameless RSPCA inspector knocked on my door, there would be nothing for me to hide. I would face them. With a measure of pride. I might even challenge them. Or show them Barnaby's fantastic frogs. Cloud's rock hard beauties. Shanty's concave masterpieces. And the massive improvement in Carrie – a horse that was about to be put to sleep when we took her on. They wouldn't be able to level a charge of cruelty against me because she wasn't in pain. She was ridden. And although she was ridden with care, she achieved high speeds and a very bold jump.

There was nothing to fear and everything to be proud of. The urge to hide in the woods started to ease and I began to talk about barefoot horses with a degree of confidence that my earlier self would not have recognised. My nightmare about Girlie was being replaced, too. I didn't seek fame on a personal level but started to dream about being interviewed on BBC Radio 4 by John Humphries, one of my favourites from the Today programme. For those of your not familiar, it's the Beeb's flagship radio programme for news and politics in the morning. Humphries is one of their most respected presenters. This was a top dream.

It was quite bizarre and my husband would have preferred if my thoughts found another direction. In my dream, Humphries was quizzing me about horse shoes and the harm they caused. The Government's Chief Veterinary Officer was also there. He was on the defensive because I was explaining to the avid listeners that the hoof was flexible and so it was harmed by the nailed-on shoe. The horse's life was being shortened. Mr Humphries understood immediately. He joined in the attack and demanded to know why the veterinary profession hadn't put its weight behind the barefoot movement.

'Clearly, shoeing is a cruel practice,' Mr Humphries insisted. 'How can you defend it?'

The Chief Vet looked pale and took a moment to find his voice. We were wearing those big earphones and he clutched his with one hand.

'Unfortunately, they are necessary. A lot of horses can't manage without them. And claims that they shorten life are not proven. It is merely conjecture.'

Humphries was straight in. 'You dispute the flexibility of the horse's foot then?'

I loved that this famous, tough interviewer had gone straight for the jugular. It was the crux of the issue and he knew it but of course it was a dream and I seemed to be in control.

'No. No, I don't but…the horse manages far better with the demands made on him if he's wearing shoes. I accept it's a compromise but so many riders have been lured by this ideal of having their horse barefoot. They hear that it's natural but there's nothing natural about us riding the horse. Sadly, many horses have been caused a lot of pain when their shoes are taken off. That is not something a vet can support.'

The interviewer turned to me. He said something. He asked me a question and he wasn't smiling. It took a moment but I finally responded.

'Taking the shoes off isn't easy,' I said, liking that my voice didn't falter. 'Some horses are uncomfortable but we are learning to minimise that. It would be such a help, though, if the vets were behind us. At the moment, owners often meet with hostility.

'I understand that as a profession you are against inflicting unnecessary pain on the horse and yet you actively support the practice of racing them when they are babies. Many die on the race course before their bones are fully formed and their feet are not full grown. At least, any discomfort in the transition to barefoot has a greater goal than the pockets of the betting industry.'

There's no studio audience present for the recording of the Today programme but in my dream there was clapping, there were cheers. It felt good to be this confident even if only in my imagination.

There was a growing number of qualified barefoot trimmers in the UK and it was still unusual for an owner to trim their own horses' feet. I was unlikely to meet with widespread approval. Thanks to the Internet it was obvious that the attitude was very different in the United States where it was hard to find a trimmer on your doorstep.

When I first had the shoes taken off my horses Dr Strasser seemed to be the only one leading the barefoot horse movement. But there were others. One was Jaime Jackson in the US. He was a traditional farrier who had become disillusioned with his trade, was convinced it was harmful and set about changing his methods.

He studied the wild horses of America, the Mustangs, and observed how they moved as a herd. He sometimes got to see their feet which were perfectly equipped for the job. They were tough, bevelled around the hoof wall and fabulously concave. Their frogs were large and tough. They looked like nothing a farrier would see in any livery yard in any country of the world. He developed a natural horse trim and I devoured every word on his website.

How would my horses fare with his trim? I liked his approach, his respect and was impressed that he found few horses needed much time off work once their shoes were pulled. It had to be good if horses were comfortable on their own feet more quickly. Few riders would tolerate bouts of tender footedness and many would have put shoes back on Barnaby when faced with his first impression of a horse wearing skis. How many would get off Carrie and lead her over the rough bits of terrain – after more than a year without shoes? It was impossible to convince riders that barefoot was a good thing if their horses were uncomfortable for more than a couple of minutes. Dr Strasser had started me on this journey but I was heading for another path – one that might meet with less resistance from the horse community.

There was a trimmer in the next county who had trained with Jaime Jackson. Carrie's troubled feet were given over to Alicia Mitchell's care for a few months. She recommended some new supplements and visited every three weeks. Oil on her feet was also suggested – first thing in the morning while they were still brushed with morning dew. If you heard the sound of crowing that would be my husband who was right all along. Who would credit it? I bought some cheap vegetable oil and added my own innovation. Tea tree oil would help prevent bacteria entering the cracks in her hooves so a few drops were added.

It's not for me to discuss the merits and differences between the barefoot trims in the market place but this one was appealing. Jaime Jackson's method seemed less invasive than others out there and my horses did well on it.

Alicia came on a tour of my fields and made all the right noises. She was particularly excited about one field that had electric fencing separating the middle. It might have been a large exercise arena but was actually a place you could put a greedy black and white cob when there were acorns on the ground. They're poisonous but he cherished them and would make himself ill so he had to be away from the oak trees that bordered every single field.

'You've made a Paddock Paradise,' Alicia said.

It was a nice name, it certainly sounded complimentary but I had no idea what she was talking about.

She explained. 'Jaime Jackson's book. Haven't you heard about it? He suggests making paddocks like this so the horses walk around the edge. I'll lend you a copy.'

There seemed to be a pattern going on with me and books. This one wasn't as dramatic as Dr Strasser's shocker but it also made so much sense. Paddock Paradise was Jackson's name for a grazing system that's extremely simple and easy to do thanks to the flexibility of electric fencing. I decided to try it with their summer field which is large and hilly and visible from my kitchen window. We used thin wooden fence posts because Barnaby always trashed the plastic ones and we bought reel after reel of tape. Help was needed with the fence posts but isn't that what families are for? My husband and my son, Max, pitched in and we had the project completed after a few sessions.

Put simply, we made what looked like a race horse gallop around the perimeter of the field. It was important to make it wide enough for horses to pass each other but it meant they would move as a herd. Jackson had observed how wild horses follow each other in a line; they are constantly on the move, picking and grazing as they go and therefore travel miles every day. That's why wild horses are fit and healthy and never need their feet trimming.

I'll never forget the first time we let them onto their rearranged field. They belted around for two circuits, bucking excitedly. It was wild and we kept out their way. Gradually they calmed down and began to graze. After a few days I could see how much they were moving from my observation post, also known as the kitchen sink.

It was incredible. One minute they were at the top of the field having a nosh; the next minute they were down the hill eating the trees. You only had to leave the window to boil a kettle and you'd return to find they were somewhere else. I should have had a device to clock their miles but can only recount how much they appeared to be constantly on the move.

Alicia had put a pedometer on one of her horses and it gave her a reading of how many steps the animal had taken. She estimated they were moving at least double the amount they would in a conventional paddock. Looking at mine, made me think it was more. This was an interesting spectator sport and better than anything on television but you might be asking *so what?*

Well, there were no great overnight changes but Carrie's feet started to respond. We had thrown everything in our power at the damned things and it was time they gave something back. It was painfully slow and I couldn't tell you whether it was the trim, the oil or the new track but they cracked less and they became more upright, a little more concave.

The horses' track was extended by making a link into the field that had Barnaby's acorn-free space. That meant they were also walking across stony ground for water and shelter. We had built a huge field shelter by this time and a stony yard which had a water trough in the middle. That yard was the best facility we could have ordered from the 5-star horse shop and now they could access it all year round.

It gave them somewhere dry and mud-free to be fed in the winter. I was fed up with slopping through mud because of course they poached the land by congregating near the gate at meal times and every rider knows how dangerous it is handling animals in those conditions. The yard got an extension the following year so there was plenty of room. They liked to stand there drying off and resting in the winter and in summer it was the best place to avoid the flies.

The yard toughened their feet with very little effort on my part. Most of them could canter across it. Carrie sometimes managed a trot. Her paces on the roads were particularly good this spring but she gets footy on too much grass and we have to be vigilant.

CHAPTER 11

If only I was a world-class rider. This book would then have the excitement of the show ring. I would take you through my preparation for the Olympics and show how my barefoot horse overcame the odds and beat those people clinging onto metal shoes. It would certainly prove my case but it's the stuff of dreams and is for someone else to achieve. You can judge a rider by their falls. It's not the water obstacle at Badminton for me; not even a wrongly executed move in a dressage ring that's unseated me. I'm what's known in the horse world as a happy hacker.

My most recent falls from the cob have been devastatingly simple and probably would never have happened to anyone who had joined the pony club as a girl. The horse was at a standstill for the first – my saddle slipped thanks to a loose girth – and the second was caused by riding in Welly boots. A tree branch went into one of my boots and hooked me off. I was hanging half off the side of the saddle while Barnaby looked at me in disbelief. At least he didn't run off as I finally slid to the ground. No, there's no pathos or drama in my riding abilities.

But my barefoot journey wasn't over. I managed to convince a few friends that horse shoes were harmful and many were still with me. I set up a barefoot livery yard and for a short while had eight horses to care for. It was the most tiring winter of my life and I had to give it up.

I wanted to do more to convince the world that any horse could walk on its own feet given natural living conditions. It wasn't enough that my own horses and those of a few friends were doing it. I couldn't become a trimmer; it was back breaking and running a large livery yard would send me to the knackers. There had to be something else.

I have been a journalist for most of my working life and for a few years have been writing fiction, trying to get a publishing deal. So of course...it had to be my mission to write about barefoot horses.

In the afterword of Dr Strasser's book there is an inspiring account of an English vet called Bracy Clark. He was one of the first pupils of the newly opened Veterinary College and led the first horse into its infirmary. That was in 1793 at a time when our country relied on these animals for every form of transport and yet was losing them in droves thanks to ignorance. If they were ill or injured, owners took to them to a farrier for their medical care. But farriers were untrained and horses were often butchered with fatal consequences.

I had to write Bracy Clark's story when I read that he had spent a lifetime campaigning against horse shoes. All those years ago.

From Dr Strasser I learnt that the veterinary establishment mocked his concerns and tried to suppress his work. The poor man was tormented by hostility from his peers and wrote, 'But what opposition have I met with, and from whom! That I might expect no mercy from the smiths, whose affairs I had exposed, was quite natural; but that the veterinarians, whose cause I had laboured and gained, should be made by interested knavery my greatest persecutors, was not to be believed…They condemned me unheard and without examination.'

Forgive me for being a journalist. My little nose was quivering with the intrigue of it. My mind was rattling with the vital question. Why?

More questions piled in. Bracy complained that he hadn't got on well with the head of the veterinary college. Professor Edward Coleman had apparently described him as a 'troublesome guest' while he was a student. He had warned that 'one of us must quit the college'.

They really hadn't been friends. The relationship got worse. In his books, Bracy describes what amounts to a whisper campaign against him emanating from Coleman; his controversial views on shoeing were laughed at but the attack was never to his face.

'He dared not make any open manly attack, which would have been quickly answered, he has, to his pupils in secret, used all the little arts of defamation.'

Bracy was treated unfairly by all the professors of the various veterinary colleges. He was never allowed to sell his work to the students; he was denied a platform. And yet, here we are today reinventing his findings. We are going over the same ground after 200 years and still having to prove the case that horse shoes do damage – they injure and it's quite possible that they shorten lives. We are trying to achieve this mostly without veterinary support, sometimes in the face of utter hostility, just as Bracy was.

His writing hooked me. Sometimes it made me emotional. You see, he knew then what so many people want to ignore now.

'The present system of shoeing, and its consequences, ruin such multitudes of horses, that surely the discovery of its cause cannot but be of the highest importance in the affairs of mankind; for not one in thirty of all that are raised live to see half of their natural life expended!'

He was sure that horse shoes killed. Picture me in the hushed British Library, carefully handling these very old, leather-bound manuscripts, muttering, 'Oh my God, oh my God. Why didn't they listen to you?'

The answer had to be somewhere amid all those books. I looked through some of the other titles. The one on bots and other insects was beautifully illustrated but an unwelcome distraction. His small work on how to build a wood burning stove gave me useful colour for my novel as did his advice on finding a good forge in the city. He wrote about the famous race horse, Eclipse, whose post mortem he had attended - more brilliant background material but shedding no light on his battle with Professor Coleman.

After one of my days at the British Library I came home with a smile. My husband spotted it and became curious.

'You've found out something, haven't you?' he asked, over dinner.

I was tired and ravenous but perfectly happy to tease. 'I might have done.'

'Come on,' he said. 'Why did Professor what's-his-name supress Bracy's findings?'

I finished my food and pushed away my plate. 'It was all down to his greed or as Bracy called it his open palm. He was corrupt. They didn't worry about libel in those days. He attacked the Professor mercilessly in the end.'

'Really? Was this in Bracy's book?'

'Yes, it's all there. Professor Coleman, apparently, was making a lot of money from horse shoes. He patented a few new designs and he didn't seem to worry that they crippled horses more than the ordinary ones. He put them on the horses that came to the college. Some of them suffered, according to my man.'

'That wouldn't make him rich, surely. How many would he sell?'

'I don't know but he had no interest in investigating an alternative to the conventional shoe.' Patrick didn't look convinced but I hadn't told him everything. Not yet. 'In one of his books, Bracy says that he suffered from a sort of whisper campaign for years. He bore it in silence but in the end he hit back. He said Coleman was corrupt. He was running one of the most rotten public institutions in the country. Bracy said he was pocketing the student fees – and here's the worst bit - he shortened the veterinary training course to three months.'

'How on earth would they produce a vet that quickly?'

'A dangerous thought, isn't it? Bracy claims he admitted the lowest characters whether they had any understanding of the horse, or not, all for the sake of the fee.'

'How long was Coleman in charge of the place?'

'More than forty years and according to the history books, he died rather a rich man. He was the college professor as well as Veterinary Surgeon General of the

British Cavalry. He sold his horse shoes and he sold medicines. He was charming, popular with his poorly educated students and very powerfully connected. It's not surprising that he wouldn't want someone like Bracy near the college, let alone trying to influence the students.

'Unlike Coleman, Bracy refused to patent any of his discoveries including some sort of flexible shoe that he made. He would publish his ingredients for medicines. He wanted to share his learning.'

'He was a Quaker, wasn't he?'

'Yes and he was way ahead of his time. Can you imagine someone all that time ago calling horses *our noble and willing slave*? I don't think he could fight dirty enough. He was no match for Coleman, sadly.'

'So what shall we call this book of yours? *A Tale of Two Horse Shoes?*'

Ah, he was laughing at me, admittedly in an indulgent way, but I could see he was having trouble envisioning this battle as the subject of a novel. Max was picking at his food and nodding his head in agreement.

I looked to Amber for support. She sniggered. 'Yeah, Johnny Depp in the film role, Mum? I don't think enough people will be interested, to be honest.'

I had the world to convince but would have to start with my family. 'Well I wouldn't make it a book about vets and horses' toe nails. Even I would find that extremely dull. No, I will make it a love story. I'll give them some adventures.'

'They could fight over the same lady,' Max suggested. 'Yuk!'

'Something like that, love. But it will have to be good. I mustn't let him down. He's my hero and it's time he was heard once more.

AFTERWORD

A Barefoot Journey opens 15 years ago. Today, it is much easier for owners to successfully take the shoes off their horse and ride barefoot.

It's brilliant that many farriers have seen the wisdom of barefoot or they are following this growing market trend and supporting clients who are riding without metal. There are many more specialist trimmers and so it is possible to get the advice and support needed.

Support and information are vital to success and if you are thinking of taking your horse barefoot you will find the Barefoot Horse Owners Group on Facebook a great source of help from thousands of members. Or there's my blog which features interviews and articles – www.nakedhorse.org.uk.

Going barefoot can still be a difficult journey to take on your own, especially if you are at a conventional livery yard seeking a natural life for your horse. I hear of people who face criticism and derision; some that are told they are cruel. But support is out there! There are more and more natural horse livery yards that allow horses to live out 24/7 in fields or tracks where their health and feet benefit from the constant movement.

* * *

An update on my horses - sadly, Shanty passed away a few years ago. Barnaby and Cloud died two years ago. All enjoyed happy retirements and excellent feet.

Carrie is still with me. She's retired and no longer the herd leader. Her feet look the best yet and it seemed only fitting that the mare who had challenged my skills so much should be my cover star. The cover photo shows me with Carrie at the top of a rocky outcrop near home. She's notorious for nudging with her head; one push and I might have been sent over the edge.

Fortunately, she didn't let me down.

ABOUT THE AUTHOR

Linda Chamberlain is the author of The First Vet, a
historical romance inspired by the life and work of Bracy
Clark. She has been a journalist most of her working life
but has ridden horses for quite a lot longer and when
she's not typing away on her latest manuscript it's because
she's off on that horse again! The First Vet combines her
love of drama with her passion for horses. She lives in
Sussex with her family and three four-legged friends who
feature largely in her popular blog –
www.nakedhorse.org.uk

ENJOY THE OPENING CHAPTER OF
THE FIRST VET

Camden, near London, 1794

Someone had to challenge the man. The governors, the other students – none of them listened to me but Professor Coleman would have to if I could bring myself to accuse him. I couldn't prove he was corrupt, he was too clever for that, but I followed him once, I saw him put the money into his own pocket.

The wind carried my voice as I rehearsed what I would say to the man who ran this place with an iron fist. The short journey from the veterinary college to his house was made difficult by the clouds obscuring the moon and I stumbled on the uneven ground. I stopped and steadied my breathing. I walked on, with more care this time.

I turned into St Pancras Way, saw the house and knew I couldn't waver. I would have to speak my mind but how to dress it up without offence? Perhaps, it didn't matter. I had nothing to lose. Every day there were rumours of bankruptcy and I feared having to return to my brother's with no qualifications and little hope. And to think, I'd given up a promising career in surgery to be here.

My hand gripped the knocker hard but I had to clear my throat when I asked the maid for Professor Coleman. She showed me to his sitting room and I was welcomed by its overwhelming heat and his very broad smile.

He shook my hand with such warmth and yet he must have been dismayed to see me. We were hardly friends. 'Clark, my dear boy! What an unexpected pleasure,' he said with far more charm than necessary. His damp hand was withdrawn from mine with such speed that I knew he was apprehensive. 'Do come in. Such a fearful night, is it not?'

'Thank you. Indeed...indeed it is.' I joined him where he

stood by the fire. He was a man of medium height but I dwarfed him and he took a step back. 'You must have known…expected me, surely. Professor…I hope you don't mind my catching up with you in this way only you've cancelled so many appointments, I began to fear you were avoiding me.'

'Oh, tut, tut, why would I make such an effort?' he sighed, leaning on the mantel and examining his long fingers. 'I would first have to notice you, would I not? Come now, I'm teasing but of course it's an honour to see any of my students at this late hour and my door is always open. I hadn't thought to extend the privilege to my home…but why not?' His eyes took their time assessing me, taking in my disordered hair, my unpolished boots and my carelessly tied neck cloth. 'Are those top boots? For the evening?' He shook his head wearily and exhaled. 'Oh, never mind, I digress.'

'Professor! What do my boots matter…when you…? Oh, you preside over the college, sir, and you must know that today something happened that concerns me greatly.' The smile hadn't shifted and he waited as I calmed my irritation. 'Well, I was told not to order any more copper of sulphate for the dispensary. I could hardly believe it. There must be a mistake.'

He coughed to cover his amusement but I could see his look of relief that I had called about something as insignificant as a shortage of medicines.

'Really? How distressing,' he said, happily. 'Give me a note about that tomorrow and I will look into it. So diligent…but I can assure you tomorrow will be early enough.'

'It keeps happening, sir. We can't treat our patients without the medicines we need. It never used to be like this. I ran that dispensary after Monsieur St Bel died and I made sure we never ran out.'

'Indeed,' he said, one eye quivering at my mention of his predecessor, a Frenchman who was as skilled at the veterinary arts as Coleman was ignorant.

'Surely the college has enough money to buy something so essential and what if one of the horses were to die as a result of this ridiculous policy.' I stopped pacing and rejoined him by the fire. 'These medicines are not expensive.'

'Not expensive!' he cried, then moderated his voice. 'If you had to buy them from your own pocket you would know they were and you wouldn't want students wasting them all the time. But if Mr Clark requires me to investigate he must give me a list. Tomorrow. Surely, you didn't venture out on a night like tonight just to tell me this.'

'The wind is blustery, nothing more. You will look into it, then?'

'I have said so. The dispensary will be stocked with the essentials.'

Ah, the essentials. He'd made me an empty promise and we would be fighting over the meaning of that word until I graduated but I had to let it go for now. I had something far more serious on my mind - if only I could find another word for corruption, one that didn't sound so dishonest.

'There is another thing, Professor.'

'You relieve my mind.'

No, there was no other way of saying it, so instead I asked him, 'Is it true that we are to give up the lease on the fields? Quite an extraordinary thing for a veterinary college to have no pasture for the horses in its care. It seems we are soon to be a laughing stock.'

He was brushing at specks of ash on his sleeve and paused only for a moment. I was skirting around the issue that plagued me but I surprised him and he exhaled slowly as if he was preparing to walk in tight boots.

'Where did you hear such a thing?' he asked. 'Rumours run through the college quicker than dysentery, do they not?'

'It's true, then?'

'No, the governors have to look at all the options and it won't be up to me in any event. But why should a young man like you worry about some fields? Why can't you be like the others and find distraction in the nearest tavern?'

He was laughing in that indulgent way he had but there was nothing kind about the suggestion. The college was run like a monastery and the hours and the rules were so strict that two students had already been thrown out. Doubtless he hoped I would obligingly get myself drunk and then expelled.

With his short, dark hair and pale face, the Professor looked older than his years but he was in his prime, young to take charge of the college. I was twenty three but the gulf between us was greater than years. I knew little of his background beyond his medical training but the luxury of the room only confirmed my suspicions. Goodness, we were cut from different cloth.

The carpet beneath my feet was thick and luxurious - deep enough to hide a thousand lies. From the dim light of the candles I could see the room was elegant. No draught ruffled the sweeping velvet drapes, no chill hung about the room which was such a contrast to our Spartan conditions at the college. A fine painting of a race horse hung above the fireplace and reminded me of the reason for my visit. How pathetic I was. How far short I had fallen from the challenge of my imaginings. The lines I had rehearsed lodged in my throat and the pause was awkward. He wouldn't tolerate me in his sitting room for long and I had to keep him talking. About anything. Until the moment was right. Oh, if only I had proof.

'I have no interest in the tavern and you know it.' I closed my eyes. I couldn't get angry. 'Sir, we shouldn't be in this mess, facing closure. Not with so many new students. You say it's only rumours but, if we are thinking of giving up the fields, it appears to be true.'

'Nonsense,' he bit out, still restrained. 'The college won't close. The government will back us; they have to.'

My hands clenched. 'We shouldn't have to grovel to the politicians not when we have such an income. It's shameful. We have hundreds of subscribers paying us to treat their horses and all your new recruits. Damn it, where are the fees going to, Professor?'

There! I'd said it. And now I only needed to look at his face to find the truth. And yet he was smiling. Not a happy smile, of course, more the weary look you'd give an irritating child you weren't ready to smack. There was a vein on one of his temples that stood out in moments of tension and even in this light I could see it.

'What are you implying?' he hissed, before glancing over his shoulder. 'The fees are not your concern. Stick to your studies, Clark. I gave you all an essay on the respiratory system to write and it won't do to get behind, you know.'

'It's written.'

I wouldn't be diverted and waited, watching him. He knew what I was suggesting even though I'd stopped short of accusing him.

'How dare you ask me about the fees in this way?' he said quietly. Had I not been standing so close, I wouldn't have heard.

'It's my duty to do so.'

'Your duty is to pass your exams and get the hell out of this college. Something you should do with ease. From the moment I was appointed, you've been trouble.'

He was remembering the time he examined the wrong leg on a lame horse. It's more easily done than you might think but I pointed it out in front of the others and he's never forgiven me.

'Professor, I know I irritate you but I demand that you give me some explanation for the plight this college is in. You owe me that at least.'

'You demand?' he said, staring at me. 'An interesting choice of words.'

'I apologise,' I said, meeting his gaze but knowing it would be unwise to antagonise him further. There were months of studying with the man ahead of me and he was very powerfully connected. 'I would be grateful if you could explain. I gave up a lot to be here, as you know.'

'Very well,' he said, coldly taking his time, assessing whether I was worth the effort.. 'It's simple enough, after all. Have you never before realised that the founders and your very dear Frenchman didn't raise enough money? They were lamentably short if they were to build a college worthy of the name.

'The new infirmary was devilishly expensive and there was no way the student fees would pay for it. Fortunately, our income has increased considerably. So, Mr Clark, you should be thanking me for saving the place but instead you dare to come here making snide accusations.'

For a minute he made me doubt myself. Was I so influenced by my distaste of him that I saw wrongdoing where there was none? Perhaps I was being foolish but I knew in my heart how false he was. That pulse on his right temple told me how anxious I was making him and there was something else bothering me. His avaricious look every time he made a new recruit.

'If you have saved the college I would indeed thank you. But the rumours haven't ceased and we all know you are appealing to the Prime Minister for funds. I am only asking what any member of the government might query.'

A sudden rustling sound and a slight cough drew my attention to the other side of the room which was swathed in shadows. The noise came from somewhere beyond a small sofa where the Professor must have been looking at some papers, now forgotten.

It seemed we were not alone. All this time someone had been listening. No wonder the Professor was speaking in whispers but she must have heard me accuse him. For God's sake, I'd been loud enough.

Printed in Poland
by Amazon Fulfillment
Poland Sp. z o.o., Wrocław

52179875R00061